How do we deal with the dissolution of a marriage? How should a Christian handle divorce? How can the church help? These are only a few of the problems dealt with in this frank book about a most disturbing upheaval in contemporary family life.

Divorce is sometimes unavoidable. The author of **THE HURT AND HEALING OF DIVORCE** tells her personal yet universal story of love and loss, offering her hard-won insight and experience.

### Here are the rules of survival:

How to cope as a single parent; how to establish a workable relationship with an ex-mate; coping with discrimination; friends, faith, and the newly divorced; moving; finding a job; divorce laws; tax deductions and confusing legalities; loneliness, dating and remarriage. THE HURT AND HEALING OF DIVORCE should be required reading for everyone.

# The Hurt And Healing of DIVORCE

**Darlene Petri**

David C. Cook Publishing Co.
ELGIN, ILLINOIS—WESTON, ONTARIO

David C. Cook Publishing Co., Elgin, IL 60120
Printed in the United States of America
Library of Congress Catalog Number: 75-18647
ISBN: 0-912692-79-0


Special acknowledgment is made to Kregel Publications
for permission to reprint copyrighted material:

Albert Barnes. "Barnes' Notes on the New Testament."
Grand Rapids: Kregel Publications, 1962.

# CONTENTS

*To those dear friends who stood*
*by me and my children when*
*we needed them . . . and*
*who demonstrated the love of*
*Christ in so many ways.*

# Foreword

The problem of divorce within the church today continues to create considerable trauma among those who find it difficult to understand why any Christian marriage should flounder to such extremes. The problem is not that Christians don't want to understand the equally, if not more severe, devastation the divorced person experiences. But rather, the conditioned spiritual reflex that comes from the hard traditional Scriptural view of divorce seems to declare that to understand is to give endorsement to it.

Along with that comes an even more "hard line" attitude about Christian divorce which emerges in judgments such as: immaturity, a desire to be "free and swinging," an inability to "stick it out," or a "shallow or erroneous grasp of the Christian law of obedience" etc. These are cruel generalizations too often levied on Christians who go through the ordeal of marital separation, and they are all the more painful in that they come from "well meaning" Christians.

Broken lives, however, need healing as the Lord Himself would command. But to heal one must have compassion and a willingness to empathize. To get that attitude it is helpful and necessary to know the hell a divorced person goes through, especially one who is a Christian. Darlene Petri has provided here a documentary on the pain, confusion and depression a Christian divorcee experiences in her attempt to reconcile the shattering reality of a lost marriage relationship with her own sense of Christian responsibility. The loneliness and tension of raising three children without a father; the sense of despair of not perhaps ever again knowing a fulfilling relationship in marriage and the ever-present sense of being judged for not "having tried harder" are all here in this frank and moving commentary.

Through this, however, comes something else, something strikingly significant, and that is the unusual dimension of a body of Christians taking the time to care which, did, in fact, provide the healing for her broken life and gave her the will to go on with God. This, then, is not only the journey of a soul through the darkness of emotional, mental and spiritual anguish, but it is also a tremendously encouraging view of a church family who reached out to help ease her burden.

What this book says about the suffering and helplessness on the part of those who become victims of unwanted broken marriage relationships ought to alter the detached or too-often-condemnatory view many Christians have about divorced people. The author's account here does not condone divorce, but it does make its moving appeal to those who should care about the healing of those who experience it.

*Wheaton, Illinois*                    JAMES L. JOHNSON
                    WHEATON COLLEGE
                    GRADUATE SCHOOL

# 1

# A Stone's Throw Away

I'D NEVER DIVORCE MY HUSBAND, no matter what!"

I didn't expect that reaction from an old friend. For once, I was speechless as she continued: "Nothing in the world could convince me that divorce is ever right. And the Bible is very definite about that."

No use even trying to explain to her that I had done what I believed was best for my children, myself and even my former husband. Hers wasn't the first closed mind I had run into, and I was weary of trying to plead my case to others. With every ounce of self-control I could muster, I made a few casual comments, excused myself, and practically ran into the ladies' restroom. For what seemed like the hundredth time, I tried to tell myself that it didn't matter what people thought.

"You'll never convince everyone that what you did was right," my pastor once said. "So don't even

13

try. Just be yourself and try not to worry about what everyone thinks."

I struggled to put my friend's words out of my mind, but it was difficult. They hurt. . . .

Later, I pondered the absolute certainty of her words and the tone of her voice. How could she be so sure?

No one really knows what's ahead in his or her marriage.

Statistics about divorce are staggering. According to the National Center for Health Statistics in Washington, D.C., two marriages are terminated for every five new ones contracted. In many large cities, the ratio is now one out of every three.

In the spring of 1974, a total of 1,727,000 marriages and 678,000 divorces took place in the United States. This is a ratio of one divorce for each 2.56 marriages.

With statistics like this, every family in America may be touched in some way — through their own divorce, or that of their parents, children, grandchildren, friends, or neighbors.

My own divorce was included in those statistics five years ago. Yet, 20 years ago, I stood next to my husband at the altar and pronounced my wedding vows, sincerely and prayerfully, in a church overflowing with friends and relatives. I took very seriously the words, "No man therefore must separate what God has joined together." I put all my hopes, dreams and ambitions into marriage. But our marriage had two strikes against it: we were very young (I was 17), and my husband had a problem which we hadn't yet diagnosed: the heartbreaking disease called alcoholism. Even so, I certainly never imagined we would end up in a divorce court.

Divorce is not something one becomes adjusted to very quickly. My transition from a homemaker and mother to a divorced head of a household wasn't an easy one. I found myself thrust headlong into an entirely different life-style and playing a totally different role. Sometimes I wasn't sure just who I was anymore, or how I fit into society.

Most people automatically assume you are one of a pair. At a school meeting, other parents will ask where my husband is. When I order children's clothing from a catalog sales store, the salesgirl always requests my husband's first name. If I apply for credit, stores are mostly interested in information about my husband's occupation. I have become more sympathetic with certain views of women's liberationists since I have been divorced. While I disagree with many aspects of the movement, I do understand what they are talking about.

Once I phoned about a note posted on a supermarket bulletin board. It was advertising a camper-trailer for sale. I happened to have a catalog describing that brand of camper in my hand when I called, so I was very familiar with the model being offered for sale.

Yet the woman who answered my call kept saying things like, "When your husband comes to look at it," or, "Your husband will appreciate how easy it is to put up," and "Your husband will recognize what good condition it is in." I didn't bother to explain

15

that I was making the decision, but I felt somewhat offended by her assumption that I had a husband.

My pastor has cautioned me, "Don't label yourself." But it is difficult to avoid doing so when you recognize that others usually put you into a separate category, apart from "regular" families.

I believe my children and I are a family. Yet, even teachers occasionally assume that when a pupil is from a "broken home" he will automatically turn out to be a problem, and maybe even a delinquent. Of course, sometimes that is the case, but many single parents work very hard to provide a good home. Maybe they even put more effort into it than some two-parent families.

Even after six years, I still have a rough time saying the words "I'm divorced." One can never predict the other person's reaction. Sometimes it's "You are?" or "Really?" Other times it's a knowing "Oh, I see." Once in a while it's an understanding "Oh, I've been divorced, too. I know what it's like."

I remember the day my family moved to the town where we presently live. A young mother came over to welcome us. It was such a friendly gesture, but I held my breath when she asked, "And what does your husband do?" — that uncomfortable question which I have come to dread.

"Well, I'm divorced," I replied.

"Oh!" As usual, an abrupt end to the conversation. In this case, my new neighbor was just embarrassed and didn't really know what to say next. I realized she was also disappointed. She and her husband had been good friends with the couple who had moved out of our house. I felt bad that she was disappointed. No, my incomplete family couldn't be a substitute for their friends who had moved away. Incidents like this sometimes leave me with an up-in-the-air feeling: I feel bad for them and for us. I also get the feeling that I am of less value because I am only half of a couple.

I get that same feeling when I attend weddings where the seats are arranged by twos, or when I am aware I create a problem for a hostess. Sometimes she doesn't really know whether or not to invite me to a get-together. If she does invite me, then she may not be sure of what to do with me when I get there. It is important for divorced people to keep positive mental attitudes so that they do not allow these incidents to affect their self-esteem.

I find it even more difficult to identify with the label "divorcee." I don't feel like the type of person the word implies. Even in our sophisticated, modern society, that word conjures up an assortment of uncomplimentary ideas in many people's minds. Divorced persons are often presumed to be irresponsible, poor financial risks, unconcerned about their children's education and welfare, and of questionable morals.

Divorce is a crisis situation, but it need not be synonymous with disaster. It is, however, probably the only situation in which one might have to adjust abruptly to a new life-style without the approval and support of family and community.

As tragic and possibly unexpected as the death of a spouse may be, the mate and any children left behind are usually surrounded by sympathetic supporters.

Yet, when a dead marriage is put to rest, the survivors often discover that society gives them neither approval nor support. They may also discover that few friends stick around to encourage them.

Upon the loss of a loved one, most bereaved persons go through a series of stages in dealing with their grief. A newly divorced person experiences similar stages upon the death of his marriage. Few suddenly-single persons fail to go through a variety of emotional, spiritual and even physical cycles. Feelings of guilt, loneliness, hostility, fear, self-criticism and loss of self-worth are included in the potentially destructive emotions. These must be worked out before the person can again be whole and secure.

A divorced person may become obsessed with a strong sense of failure. He may lose his normally positive self-concept; instead he may begin to feel and act like a "loser." Sometimes his preoccupation with the past prevents his working toward a new life.

His loss is of a much different nature than that of a widowed person. The engulfing grief usually accompanying the death of a mate is heightened by the knowledge that death brings the end of marriage, a marriage which may have been good and meaningful and exciting.

Whether a marriage is ended by divorce, death or desertion, if there are children involved, the suddenly-single parent finds himself facing enormous adjustments as well as the responsibility of providing a stabilizing influence on the children. Decisions must be made alone which previously were made with the help of the marriage partner. This in itself can be an overwhelming experience.

National census data indicates there are over 11 million widowed persons, the large majority being women. Since divorced women are still awarded child custody more often than men (although the pendulum is changing in this direction; see chapter 5), it is a statistical fact that most heads of single-parent families are women.

Women, especially, may face great financial difficulties. The late husband may have failed to provide sufficient life insurance. A divorce court may have decided on a meager child-support figure. If a woman has been deserted by her husband, she may be faced with the choice of going to work and paying out much of her earnings for child care or deciding to collect welfare payments and lose what dignity she feels she has left.

Death also differs from divorce or desertion by its very irrevocability. There is not that possibility of remarriage or hope that a missing mate will return. In divorce or desertion these question marks can remain as open wounds which do not heal as quickly as wounds caused by the clean, sharp cut of death.

Feelings of failure and acute awareness of unmet needs can cause a divorced person to wonder whether he made a mistake. Things don't seem to have been all that bad, now that he looks back at the situation. Being lonely can cause normally sensible persons to lose their objectivity. (These feelings are most acute during the first year after divorce and usually de-

19

crease after that. If after that time a person is still wondering whether it was a mistake, it might help to sit down and make a list of the problems which caused the breakup.)

What one really may be missing is the *state* of marriage: the habit of doing things routinely, the companionship of going places together. These probably provided a security of a sort, no matter how intolerable the marriage became.

I went through a period of doubt shortly after I left my husband. I realized that he did love his children and was having a rough time accepting the fact that they would not be living with him anymore. I felt sorry for all of us, and this was haunting me.

The more I dwelt on it, the weaker I became. I knew I had to talk to someone about the situation, someone knowledgeable about our particular problem of alcoholism. I went to an alcoholic rehabilitation center and talked with a counselor. I explained to her my feelings of uncertainty and my fear that I would weaken in my decision if my estranged husband put enough pressure on me.

First she made it very clear that "We are here to help save marriages, not encourage their breakup. But each situation is unique. Some marriages never should have taken place in the first place." (I believe mine was one of those.)

She encouraged me to think objectively by reminding me: "Count noses. You have three children and yourself to consider. You are perfectly justified in removing them from such a disturbing situation. Of course you are disappointed that you have been unable to help your husband overcome his drinking problem. But your entire family does not need to remain in such an unhealthy and unhappy situation. If your spouse had a contagious disease, would you allow your children to be exposed to it just because you didn't want to hurt his feelings? Would it help him if his children caught the disease?"

She also made me face up to my tendency to play a martyr role. She stated emphatically, "It is very likely that you will *never* be the one to help your husband. And it doesn't help a bit for you to remind him, 'Look at all I've gone through because of your drinking. I've worked hard and devoted years to our marriage.' Making him feel guilty won't help a thing, and he won't believe you anyway."

One word stuck out in my mind as I was driving home from the rehabilitation center. The word "detached." The counselor had stressed that mental attitude. It wouldn't be easy to become detached from the father of my children, but I knew she was right. I had to at least work at it.

After that, I had more confidence in my decision. I never weakened again.

A successful divorce requires adequate mental and spiritual preparation. Survival is easier if one can anticipate the emotional and physical turmoil divorce creates. Then that person will be better able to face the variety of situations and emotional upheaval that lies ahead.

Gale Sayers was a strong support to his friend Brian Piccolo when Piccolo was dying of cancer. Sayers was in the room when Piccolo was told he

21

would need surgery on newly discovered tumors. Sayers took the hospital administrator aside, urging him to give Piccolo time to get used to the situation. He said, "When we athletes get ready for a game, we have to prepare mentally as well as physically."

It's that way with divorce. And even with mature preparation and sensible preplanning, divorce is never easy.

One of the most difficult aspects of divorce is establishing a different relationship with an ex-spouse. It is practically impossible to live with a person for years and then abruptly cut off any feelings for that person.

A divorce decree and a trip to court do not automatically end a relationship. During the years you live with your mate, you share material possessions, set goals, dream dreams, experience emotional and sexual closeness and enjoy mutual friends. It is difficult if not impossible to immediately sever all these emotional ties. Even when these bonds have become uncomfortable ropes, binding each other, tying knots around each other, they are still strong.

You can't help occasionally wondering how your ex-mate is doing, or what he is feeling. You aren't sure whether to send a birthday greeting. You want to tell him when mutual friends experience a family crisis.

In his book, *Emotional Common Sense,* author Rolland S. Parker states:

It is useful to explore why the breakup of an important relationship occurred. There is an overwhelming tendency to blame the other person. At the minimum, however, you either encouraged or permitted that relationship. There was likely some blind spot, some lack of self or social understanding which prevented you from understanding your needs or those of the other person. It is also likely that you were active in spoiling the relationship. You must explore what you did to provoke the other person's anger or dissatisfaction. I find that when people complain about a particular characteristic in another person, they are likely to show this themselves.

It is possible that as the individual and his/her mate lived together, one or both developed in ways that could not be predicted at the time of marriage, or one of them matured and the other stagnated or regressed.

Individuals react differently to the breakup of an intense meaningful relationship. Some avoid people, others need contact but cannot stand sex, still others want sex but can't stand commitment, and some immediately want to remarry.

I do not believe there is any such thing as an "innocent party" in a divorce situation. Of course, the breakup of a marriage usually comes as a result of certain major problems or conditions, such as cruelty, infidelity, excessive gambling or drinking, or a major blowup. But even a person backed up against something as destructive as an alcoholic spouse is bound to make some pretty serious mistakes. I sure did.

I lost my temper (yes, in front of my children), I was critical, I played the martyr role, and I rescued him from financial problems he should have been forced to face — all traits (I later learned through education about alcoholism) which do more harm than good to an alcoholic as well as to the family.

Yet, I receive more sympathetic support than many other divorced persons, because I am considered "the innocent party." Sometimes I feel uncomfortable about that.

I remember a minister whose wife worked for the same publisher I previously worked for. He felt it was his business to give me the third degree about my marital status. Finally he said, "Well, it's all right then. In a case like yours, it is acceptable for you to leave. Of course, you realize it would not be acceptable for you to get remarried."

He had come to the conclusion that he could more or less give me some approval on my divorce because he was convinced I was the "innocent party." I liked this man as a person and didn't debate the subject. But suppose he had not felt convinced of my "innocence"?

I believe the people who demonstrate true Christianity are the ones who accept me, no questions asked — just as I am.

A similar situation came to my attention recently. A book written by a divorced mother of three was reviewed in a Christian magazine. The reviewer made an obvious point of stating that the book was by "a blameless mother of three." I read the book and I believe the author would agree with me: no one is blameless in a breakup. One mate might contribute more to the problem, but both make mistakes.

Tragically, it usually takes months and even years after a marriage breakup to regain enough objectivity to see your own flaws. Then you feel sorry all over again because of the things you might have done to improve your marriage.

It is difficult for friends of a divorced couple to avoid taking sides. I was fortunate because most of my friends remained friends with both my former husband and me.

Sometimes things look very different to those on the outside than to those in the middle of a breakup. But this problem isn't unique to modern society. A Roman divorced from his wife was being highly blamed by his friends, who demanded: "Was she not chaste? Was she not fair? Was she not fruitful?"

Holding out his shoe, he asked them whether it was not new and well made. "Yet," he added, "none of you can tell where it pinches me." (Plutarch in *Aemilius Paulus.*)

It is very important for a divorced person to establish a workable relationship with an ex-mate, especially if there are children involved. This isn't easy, but neither is it impossible. And in the long run the result is well worth the effort.

Facing reality is the first step — accepting the situation as it is, not the way you hoped it would be, or the way it "should have been."

After a couple divorces, they may be surprised at their reaction to each other. They might find out that they like each other as long as they are not living together.

Too often, one ex-mate entertains unrealistic hopes of a reconciliation, or even refuses to accept the fact that the divorce actually took place. While there is that possibility of reconciliation, most people are merely building fantasies and refusing to recognize the permanence of the divorce. A casual comment made by one's former spouse may become enlarged and misconstrued in a person's mind. Words said in everyday conversation can be twisted to have a double meaning. This is an especially damaging situation when children are caught up in it, hoping against hope for their parents' reconciliation. Refusing to let go hurts everyone.

Sometimes one ex-mate actually promotes the other's hopes for reconciliation by playing a game.

Carol helped put Larry, her husband, through college by working as a legal secretary. It was a long financial struggle until he finally graduated. Just prior to graduation, Carol found she was pregnant. Two additional children followed, so that during the beginning years of his new career they continued to live under considerable financial stress.

In time, his position advanced so that finally they were able to purchase a lovely home. Shortly thereafter they enjoyed their first real vacation. Finances were no longer a real problem.

In conjunction with his climb up the ladder of success came considerable out-of-town travel, late meetings and much socializing. At first Larry insisted that his wife accompany him on most of his business trips, and they left the children with his parents. After a while, Larry stopped encouraging her to go with him, but Carol did not suspect an ulterior motive. So it was a real jolt when Larry broke the news that he was in love with his young secretary.

Carol resisted at first and attempted to fight for her husband. She was so crushed by the irony of the fact that after they worked so hard together during the tough years, now when they were reaching their goals, the marriage was falling apart.

Eventually she gave him a divorce and he did marry his secretary. But from time to time he still comes around to see her. He becomes very complimentary and even tells her how much he misses her.

This is playing havoc with Carol's emotions. "Am I going to get him back?" she wonders. "Would I even want him back now? Could I live with the fact that he might, at any time, find another romance?"

Chances are, Carol is worrying unnecessarily. More than likely, Larry is playing a game with her. He is building up his ego by the fact that he has his choice of two women. He wants his ex-wife to continue to love him, so he ignites any smoldering sparks whenever possible.

A relationship like this is destructive to everyone involved. His new wife doesn't appreciate his visits to his ex-wife, and the children are entertaining hopes that their parents might remarry.

This is a difficult situation for Carol. She must be objective and that isn't easy.

On the other hand, a divorced couple may develop unhealthy attitudes toward each other which can become destructive to themselves and the children. It is only too common to hear of cases where a hostile divorced person continues to persecute his ex-mate long after the divorce is final. Some people deliberately attend gatherings where a former partner will be because they want to feel injured. Jealous ex-mates have made headlines by spying on their former husband or wife, possibly even becoming violent.

"Life is a struggle, but not a warfare," said John Burroughs. That applies so well to divorce; it might be a struggle but should not be a warfare.

Sometimes a divorced person has a compulsion to check up on her former spouse to find out details of any new romances. This is especially true when the spouse was the one who initiated the divorce. This might be jealousy because someone else now has him and she thinks she's missing something. Or it may be just because she hasn't any romance at the moment, a reaction caused by boredom or loneliness.

Sadly, sometimes hostile divorced persons use their children as trophies to be won or tossed from side to side as a way of "getting even." The children become the real victims of their hostility.

I know of one situation where a father refuses to visit his son very often because he says, "I don't want to be used as a babysitter so my ex-wife can go bar-hopping." But whom is he punishing?

The recovery or healing process, then, is of ultimate importance as to how maturely two people are able to change roles in a relationship. The success of their reorientation and adjustment can be the determining factor as to whether the parents and children alike become permanently scarred as a result of divorce.

It is important to recognize unhealthy feelings and attitudes and get help in handling them if necessary. (See list at back of book of organizations to contact for assistance.) Destructive emotions cannot be successfully tucked away into the back of one's mind. They must be brought out, looked at objectively, tackled and dealt with constructively. Then a healthy healing process can take place, and divorce can become a springboard for a new life — a better and happier one. (There is nothing more tragic than for a person still smoldering and hurt from a bad marital experience to jump into a second marriage without first resolving and solving his inner conflicts.)

This is where the Christian community can and must enter in: In my case, it was through the support and affirmation of my church — my pastor and our congregation — that my own healing slowly but surely took place.

My church was marvelously supportive throughout my marriage and divorce. I had been discussing the situation with my pastor for years, sometimes alone and sometimes with my former husband. My pastor and his wife and many other couples from my congregation were a real strength to me. Time and time again I would plead with them, "Just tell me what to do and I'll do exactly what you recommend." Time and time again they explained that there were no pat answers — right or wrong. I had to work things out by making my own decisions. But they reassured me that their homes were open whenever I needed to talk. I felt free to call whenever I needed someone to care. I desperately needed their support, and they were always ready with it. They also recognized that since they had not been through the situation themselves, they could not totally realize the variety of emotions I was experiencing.

When, in time, I did make the decision to get a divorce, my congregation was a true example of a loving community of the body of believers. They didn't take sides but stood by me with words of encouragement and actions that backed up those words. They surrounded me with their love and acceptance. They reaffirmed my action by convincing me that they believed in me and knew I could make it with God's help. They made statements like, "You'll make it," "If anyone can do it, you can!" and "Your children will be just fine."

They not only helped me face up to and accept the situation I was in, but they helped me make realistic plans for the future. They worked at rebuilding my shattered self-image. They were a nurturing force, demonstrating the love of Christ to me in many ways.

So it was through the heartaches and headaches of marital problems and finally a divorce that I discovered what Christian friends are all about. I have been encompassed by their love. And, greater still, I have experienced the very real love of Jesus.

Because, even though I am divorced, He didn't desert me. He strengthened me, loved me, comforted me and guided me. He has forgiven me the many mistakes I made during the years of my married life. And He has been to me "a very real help in time of trouble."

And He is waiting to help anyone and everyone who seeks Him.

"Oh, praise the Lord, for he has listened to my pleadings! He is my strength, my shield from every danger. I trusted in him, and he helped me. Joy rises in my heart until I burst out in songs of praise to him" (Ps. 28: 6, 7, *The Living Bible*).

That has been my experience.

# 2

# Marriage on the Rocks

MY DIVORCE was no "snap decision." For many years I had struggled through our shaky marriage, never even seriously considering the possibility of separation, mostly because I was afraid of God's disapproval and anger. Would He desert me if I left my husband?

But day after day I lived with the terrifying feeling that I was trapped in a box. There didn't seem any way out. I was suffocating to death.

As the years passed, I began to think more realistically about the possibility of leaving my husband. That running debate was constantly in my mind, night and day. No matter what I was doing or where I was, the problems were heavy on my mind. Washing dishes, ironing, cleaning, writing, the questions were haunting me: Should I or shouldn't I leave? What is God's will? What is best for my children?

Just when I would become thoroughly convinced

that there was no other solution but for me to leave, suddenly our home life would seem to settle down. For a short while, life was tolerable. We'd actually begin to relax and enjoy each other and our home.

But, whenever there is an alcoholic in the family, there is always that realization and accompanying fear: "This won't last." It is like a temporary lull before a storm — nice while it lasts, but very misleading.

Life would run smoothly for a few days, and I'd begin to convince myself that this time it would last. This time things would be different. This time everything was going to come out okay. By the time the big blowup would come (and it always did), I'd be totally unprepared for it. Afterward, I'd wonder at my stupidity and ask myself, "How could I have not realized this would happen? It always does!"

By the end of 1969, I was beginning to face the fact that things were not going to change unless I initiated the change. How often I had prayed for my husband's healing. I also had prayed, "Lord, show me what to do." But then I'd be afraid to do anything for fear I'd act against God's will. I had to be sure I was doing the right thing. Yet, looking back, I realize that often I failed to see signs right before my eyes.

As the winter set in that last year, things looked really bad. Financially we were wiped out. Emotionally I was exhausted. I could hardly function as a mother because I was so weary.

Two years earlier, we had sold our home in a Chicago suburb to purchase a small resort in northern

Wisconsin. My husband felt that if I would leave my friends and my church, and he would get away from his drinking buddies by moving to a new area, we'd have a fresh start. Later, after I became more informed about alcoholism, I recognized that this "geographical relocation" is a popular pattern for alcoholics.

Living in the woods with few people around didn't help our marriage. The location was breathtaking and the view across the lake beautiful. Our house was on a hill, only a few feet from the lake. But now I also had the responsibility of cleaning five cabins every Saturday, taking reservations at any time of the night or day and, above all, keeping our guests happy. In addition, my own children had few friends to play with. At the time we moved there, I was expecting Danny, my third child. He was due to be born on the very day fishing season opened, an important date to resort owners. Danny cooperated by arriving four weeks early.

Among our first guests was a fun-loving couple, the Browns. They met Danny when he was only a few weeks old and nicknamed him "Dan Boone" because he was born in the north woods. Danny is still called "Boonie" by family and friends, though we now live far from the woods.

I still have memories of the lovely scenery that surrounded our home as well as of the new friends we made while living in that Wisconsin resort town. But the move did not help my husband's drinking problem or our marriage. In fact, the situation became increasingly worse.

By then, I knew I had tried everything in my power to help him. He had to want to help himself. In the meantime, I could not see any sense in all of us being destroyed. As it was, to a certain degree, our entire family had become emotionally disturbed. Alcoholism becomes a family sickness as each person tries to manipulate and blame other members of the family for the problems. Sometimes we had violent arguments. I was scared to death of what was going to happen — of how we'd all end up.

I remember becoming more and more aware that it was just a matter of time. I prayed differently by then. I pleaded, "Lord, guide me and show me what to do — and when."

I analyzed seriously the possibility of my getting a permanent full-time job. I thought about the kind of work I would want to do and started to think about where my children and I could live. Obviously, we would have to leave the woods. Not only did we live 20 miles from town, but in a tourist area where there were very few year-round jobs available at all. Also, being snowed in for days during the winter was not unusual.

As things worked out, we were spending the winter in southern Wisconsin when I finally left. After living through one long cold winter unemployed, we discovered a better way to survive the winter. Beginning in the second year, we rented a furnished home in southern Wisconsin while the owners spent the winter in Florida. Work possibilities for my husband were better there. So prior to the time I left, we had closed up the resort for the winter.

I decided to return to Illinois, within a reasonable distance from our former church and all our friends. Job opportunities would be better in that general vicinity too.

Looking back, I can see how God was guiding and directing my thoughts. He knew very well that, while we had a hard road ahead, He would be there to give us strength, protection and love.

It is ironic that, in the end, my husband and I separated on our thirteenth wedding anniversary. Of course, it wasn't just the events of that one day that caused me to finally decide, "This is it." Things had been working up to the breaking point, and by now I was pretty much convinced that there was no alternative. Our relationship was rapidly deteriorating, and the last hours were very painful.

Packing what I could in our station wagon, I headed for Illinois to my in-laws' home. I dreaded telling them the situation because they had been good to all of us. But they took us in, and we stayed there until I found a job and located an apartment.

New Year's Eve day is not the ideal time to hunt for an apartment. It's difficult enough for a woman with three children to find a place to rent. And, to further complicate the situation, I was only guessing as to the location where I'd be most likely to find a job in the publishing field.

I had very strong convictions about the type of work I'd be doing. I knew I'd be worried about my children, especially the youngest. (At this time, Pam was 11 years old, Tim was three and Dan a year and a half). I worried that he'd put his finger into an elec-

37

trical socket, fall downstairs or just be lonely for me. Also, I had a strong desire to find a job which would be creative and stimulating. Any job where I'd have extra time on my hands, or where I'd be so bored that time would drag, would give me that many more hours to worry and feel guilty about being away from my kids.

I zeroed in as to where I felt my best job possibilities would be. Later, after checking out newspaper ads and employment agencies, I gradually came to the conclusion that I would have to find another way of job-hunting than through the want ads. I prayed a great deal about finding the job that the Lord wanted me to have.

The idea of going back to work was frightening to me for many reasons. For one thing, I had few clothes which were appropriate for the working world. But I claimed a Bible verse as a constant reminder that I wasn't operating on my own power but on Christ's. "I can do all things through Christ which strengtheneth me" (Phil. 4: 13).

We were fortunate in being able to sublease an apartment where three children were allowed. It was halfway between our church and an area where a number of religious publishing houses were located.

The fact that we were subleasing it gave us less contact with the landlord and therefore less problems. At that time, I was thinking in terms of taking my children away from a bad home situation just until their dad could get help. The idea of divorce was still far from my mind.

I just knew that the situation had gotten out of

hand. I hoped and believed that with proper help and enough time, our family would be reconciled.

Since these were the circumstances, I simply told the landlord the truth: "My husband is in Wisconsin. I came down to get a job." So I didn't run into the problems I would face later when trying to rent or buy a home as a divorcee.

Meanwhile, the apartment was unfurnished and our furniture was in northern Wisconsin. I made a quick decision. Pam and I would just have to go up and get whatever we could put in a trailer.

All we had taken to southern Wisconsin with us for the winter were clothes, my sewing machine, toys and books. Everything else was up in the woods, snowbound. The gas, electricity, heat and water were all shut off. But we had to go.

Grandma and Grandpa agreed to care for the boys while Pam and I made the trip. They also provided us with some much-needed cash.

We left Sunday evening at 6:30 and drove all night. Since I have a tendency to fall asleep at the wheel when driving at night, Pam's job was to keep me awake. We drove the 425 miles, rented a trailer in town, and took a detour to stop at our friends' home for breakfast.

An earlier call to the county chairman assured me that our roads were plowed. We had paid the plowing fee before going down south. Unfortunately, he was unaware that the driver of the plow, knowing we were gone for the winter, had only plowed half-way into our property. Seeing a convenient turning point, he did just that. Therefore, when I came barreling in, trailer in tow, fast enough to get up the hill without sliding back, I had no way of realizing that suddenly the driveway would be snowbound. And had I braked I would have slid back down into a drift. So, we drove the best we could, as far as we could, up the hill toward the house. Then we were really stuck. Pam and I practically crawled up the frozen snow to the house, which was below zero inside, since it was at least 20 degrees below zero outdoors. We were exhausted already. Fortunately, our friends with whom we had eaten breakfast started worrying about us and decided to follow us. They brought hot coffee in a thermos, but that froze in the cup while we were busy trying, with frozen fingers, to unscrew the baby crib.

Finally, hours later, by unhooking the trailer and turning it by hand, backing the car down the hill, and literally sliding the furniture down the hill on a toboggan, we filled the trailer and station wagon with the most necessary items. We left tired, but sure the worst was behind us. Now, just 425 miles and we'd be home free.

Wrong. About halfway home, I began to feel my feet swelling in my boots. I took off the boots and drove with stocking feet. This eased the discomfort for a while. Pam kept watch for signs, indicating the number of miles to the next town. We'd quickly pull in for a Coke and coffee. Then we'd time our miles against the clock. We made it as close as 35 miles from our destination when suddenly the car stopped dead. I couldn't believe it.

While I was desperately attempting to get my feet

back into my boots, a squad car pulled up next to us. A policeman got out and peered into my window. He stared at my efforts as he told me he'd have to phone for a tow truck. I was about as exhausted at this point as I had ever been in my life. I could hardly stand on my feet, the pain was so bad. Later I discovered my toes were frostbitten.

No one had thought to check the gas gauge, so, when the car would not respond to a jump, it was towed to the nearest service area. There it was discovered that I was simply out of gas. In all the haste, I hadn't noticed that at the last service station where we had assumedly "filled up" our gas tank, the attendant had taken our money for a full tank but given us less than half. I tried not to burst into tears as I paid the costly towing charge and filled my gas tank.

We started on our last painful lap. Next we ran into a road construction detour and ended up miles from our destination. I began to wonder if we really would ever arrive back safely. I felt like I couldn't possibly drive another mile.

But I did. And in time, we got the trailer unloaded and my toes unthawed. My car, too, had evidently been overworked. The next day, with the trailer still attached, it wouldn't start at all.

The first morning we woke up in the apartment with our furniture now in it, I expected to feel more secure. Instead, I woke on that day with strong feelings of apprehension. Fear kept wanting to poke out its ugly head: What if I had made a mistake? After all we had been through!

Worst of all, what if I couldn't find a job? I was really afraid. But I couldn't even try to find a job just yet, for my toes were still frostbitten and I could only wear tennis shoes with the toes cut out. In addition, all three of my kids came down with sore throats and colds. My car wasn't working, my phone was not yet connected, I had little money and was taking aspirins for my own stuffy nose. I was hardly a likely prospect for a job.

As I watched my children still sleeping fitfully, I wondered if I would ever be able to provide them with the kind of security and good home that they deserved.

In my fear, I knew I had to call on the Lord for power. I knelt down at the foot of my son's bed and begged the Lord to guide me and reassure me that He would get us through this turmoil. And then it happened.

I felt as though all of a sudden a warm covering was gently being put around me — almost like being inside a warm, cozy balloon. And even better was the immediate peace that accompanied this feeling. I could feel the fear draining out of me and being replaced by peace. A Bible verse explains the comforting and reassuring experience better than I ever could: "Long ago, even before he made the world, God chose us to be his very own, through what Christ would do for us; he decided then to make us holy in his eyes, without a single fault — we who stand before him covered with his love" (Eph. 1: 4, TLB).

The next day I began making a list of job possibilities and a telephone man arrived to install our phone. One phone call led to another till finally I lined up a few interviews. Grandpa came to watch the kids and let me use his car to go job hunting.

In the back of my mind, I had believed I would find a position with a particular religious publisher, since I had read their ad for editors in *Writer's Market*. I was knocked back a few steps when I discovered they had no openings remaining in my field.

On my way back to the apartment, I passed another religious publishing house. The next day I phoned its personnel director. He connected me with the managing editor. It just happened that a day or so earlier, a young woman in the editorial department had given notice that she was expecting a baby and would be leaving — my first realization of God's perfect timing. Had I gone job-hunting before I made the trip to Wisconsin, this position would not even have been available. Time and time again, I have discovered that God's timing is so perfect.

The managing editor set up an interview for the following morning. I also had been able to make two other appointments, one that following afternoon and a second that following evening.

Now things were beginning to look more hopeful. I had a very definite job possibility. Grandpa again volunteered his car and services.

The next problem that crossed my mind was, "What can I wear?" My wardrobe, which had been sufficient for my life as a mother and resort owner, was not appropriate for a working girl. Before I even had time to worry about it, friends were at my door.

A young woman who had been in my Sunday school class asked, "Could you use this coat? I have more than I really need." Another friend loaned me her two best suits so I would be able to apply for a job feeling self-confident about my appearance. Before I knew it, there were clothes in my closet and my children's as well. (They brought along some food for my cupboard, too.)

The first appointment the next day went quite well. They would let me know for sure the following morning if they could use me, and they were not hesitant about my starting immediately. That would provide time for me to be trained before the other girl had to leave.

Proceeding on to my second appointment, I was fortunate in running into a person who recognized my lack of self-confidence and cared enough to try to help me. Though he had no position which would be available immediately, he took the time to make some helpful suggestions. He also recommended that I read the book *Psycho-Cybernetics* by Dr. Maxwell Maltz, a Christian plastic surgeon. (I did read it later and found it very helpful.)

The evening appointment also proved to be more meaningful than I had expected. This time it was Char Meredith, co-author with Bill Milliken of the book *Tough Love,* who gave me a few more spurts of confidence. She asked about my personal situation and then pointed out, "Real love *is* tough. You were not helping your husband by being so easy on him. You will help him far more by showing him that you do not plan to allow your children and yourself to be permanently emotionally disturbed by his behavior." Meeting Char Meredith was another example of how God was guiding me to loving and concerned Christians.

The next day I received a phone call from the editor at the religious publishing house. The job was mine if I wanted it, and I could begin immediately.

I couldn't believe it! I had an apartment, my furniture, and now a job. God *had* worked things out. The last problem was to find a baby-sitter. Since I didn't know anyone in that particular town, I phoned the one source I felt might have a suggestion. The friendly woman who answered the number listed in the A1-Anon newspaper ad was very helpful. She suggested I contact a former member of A1-Anon who lived nearby. When I called the woman she recommended, she told me about her next-door neighbor. By the next morning I had a great baby-sitter lined up.

Working on the editorial staff of a religious publication was challenging and meaningful. Oh, there were some problems. My car rarely started in winter, and I felt like I was nearly supporting the local service station. My children were so young that when I returned home in the evening, I had to spend a lot of time reading and playing with them as well as washing diapers. But I knew I had made the right decision. Having a job which you can look forward to going to each day makes the numerous tasks involved in simply getting there much more worthwhile.

# 3

# Working Mothers

WOMEN GETTING A DIVORCE TODAY have one thing going for them that their mothers or grandmothers didn't. This advantage probably explains the rising number of women today who are selecting divorce as the best alternative to an intolerable or miserable marriage.

Work opportunities for women never have been as challenging and numerous as they are today. Some promising careers have only recently opened up to women, such as police officers, medical technologists, and engineers.

Nondiscriminatory application forms and tests, open job positions, and equal opportunity laws passed in the 60's are making many more jobs available to women.

This means that getting a divorce need not sentence a woman to a meaningless job. Instead, divorce can open up an entirely new world to a woman who was becoming intellectually stagnant.

The three things that most often limit a divorced woman in pursuing her preferred profession are: lack of time to find the right job, children who need care and financial security, and insufficient education and/or experience.

When a woman suddenly becomes single, whether through being widowed, divorced or deserted, there is usually little time to plan a career and become properly qualified for a high-paying position. In addition to financial pressures, society usually expects her to get back into some sort of normal routine as soon as possible.

A person who has been living as a married partner naturally has been somewhat dependent on her spouse, though in varying degrees. Yet, no matter how independent and self-sufficient a wife may have been, chances are she didn't have to tinker with the furnace or learn how to adjust the carburetor. So, some very real adjustments must be made for her to adapt to the new role of a working, newly single woman.

I already have stressed the importance of searching, if at all possible, for a job that is interesting, exciting and satisfying, a job which challenges you to new plateaus of creativity. Sadly, there are those women who have few options because they are limited by their lack of education, number of children or geographical location.

Women over 40 often feel particularly concerned about barriers because of their age. But if they list the advantages and present them to potential employers, they are statistically very impressive. For example, statistics show that women over 40 are usually more dependable and have good attendance records. They stay put longer once they find a job. They also have fewer family problems: most of their children are grown or at least less dependent on them.

Some companies refuse to hire divorced women at all. Others will hire divorced women without children or those over 40. Many companies refuse to hire women who are the sole support of their children, believing they will be unreliable. Yet studies have shown that divorced women often have less absenteeism than men, since they have such a strong sense of responsibility.

With the double handicap of being a woman and divorced, it pays to do some homework ahead of time to try to find out just what the company's attitude is in the long run toward divorced women. Would you be forced to stay in the same job because it would be against company policy for a divorced woman to hold a high position?

In addition, there are special problems for divorced Christians who prefer a career in a religious organization. I was encouraged and my confidence rebuilt considerably when the board of directors of my own church hired me as a part-time youth director.

As previously mentioned, I had selected a Christian publishing company when I first needed a job. In a number of ways I was being an idealist. I felt that there I would be sheltered from the world and embraced in Christian love in much the same way as I had been by my church.

I found many wonderful friends there. They prayed with me and showed honest concern when I needed a new baby-sitter or had car trouble. Many cheered me up by taking me out to eat; others offered their husbands' services to work on my car. So, by and large, I have good feelings about that experience.

But there were also a few employees who were very judgmental of divorced persons. Their attitude was an obvious put-down. This came as quite a jolt to me, and if I had not already experienced the encouragement of my own pastor and friends, I might have become very disillusioned.

So this is another important consideration in selecting a job: do you want the boundaries and yet the challenge of working for a Christian organization, or the less legalistic viewpoints of the secular world?

I am presently very content in my position as editor of a religious publication. This company was willing to take the risk that somewhere, sometime, an ultraconservative reader might discover the editor is divorced and cancel his subscription. I am grateful for my company's open-mindedness.

Some Christian publishers won't hire divorced persons at all. Of the many attitudes toward divorced women, the most relentless and unfair is the moralistic. Although it isn't spelled out in clear-cut words, there is usually the implication that a divorced person did something wrong.

I worked temporarily for one religious organization

while they searched for a permanent replacement. The supervisor, pleased with my efforts, said, "It's too bad you're divorced, because otherwise we'd hire you." Of course, the policy was not set by this woman and I understood that. As a matter of fact, she called another religious publisher to see if they were hiring editors. However, they, too, discriminated against divorced persons. I didn't tell this woman that I knew I could never have survived such a closed-minded environment, even had they offered me the position. But my defense mechanisms were hard at work and I had a difficult time returning the next day.

A job should accomplish a number of things: supply income, provide a sense of accomplishment, give status and bring out creative abilities. However, of the more than 5.5 million widowed, divorced or separated women working in 1968, almost all held jobs primarily because it was a financial necessity.

Over 12 percent of American families are now headed by women, and studies show that by 1980 the number of families headed by women will have almost doubled. It already has gone up 50 percent since 1960.

Average women heads of household are in their early 30s, and they are usually divorced. Statistics have reversed, since in 1960 there were more widowed heads of households.

Many newly single women are lacking in self-confidence when they first reenter the business world. No matter which of the marital partners initiates the divorce, in the end both parties may suffer guilt feelings and sharp blows to their self-confidence. This is another reason it can be meaningful to become established in a job with long-range potential and a fulfilling experience. The status that sometimes accompanies a career can do great things for a woman's punctured ego. It can change her "label." Instead of being referred to as "a divorcee," she may now be referred to as an educator, social worker, etc. While a man is almost always labeled according to his profession, a woman is more often labeled according to her marital status.

There is an unconscious tendency for society to think in these terms. Until a woman becomes divorced herself, she usually has not been aware of this subtle prejudice. A person's consciousness of her own divorce makes her especially aware of that tendency.

For example, in a recent election, newspapers reported, "A 30-year-old 'divorcee' announced her candidacy." The same newspaper referred to a "successful lawyer who is running for office" without mentioning that he was also divorced.

Obviously a double standard — disapproval of the woman's status of divorce but failure to even mention when a male candidate has been divorced. In addition, her divorce was used as counterweight to an opposing candidate's brush with scandal. Many an unthinking voter considered divorce in the same category as immorality. The question posed by *Newsweek* magazine in discussing it was: "Which offends voters more — the actuality of the female's divorce or the suggestion of male philandering?"

When a woman has come to grips, then, with the

barriers she might face in job-hunting, the next step is to work out a resume. This is a concise, factual written record of who you are and what you have done. It can be included with a letter when you contact an employer by mail or taken to a job interview. (See your library for specific books on job application and resumes.)

It also is helpful to make out a personal list of what you feel constitutes the ideal job. Then study want ads and pamphlets and books on occupations to find out what is available.

Many colleges can be of help in informing women of job possibilities. They provide tests which help determine in what career the person's abilities would be put to best use and for which jobs they are best suited.

Sometimes it is advisable to work for a temporary office service while finding a permanent job. This can be worthwhile, not only because of the time which it allows for further job-hunting, but for the experience, brushing up, and adjustment for reentry into the business world.

It also will give you an opportunity to see firsthand a variety of offices and businesses. You may discover you'd enjoy a completely different line of work than you were originally considering. It also can help you determine the jobs you wouldn't want on a permanent basis. You may have felt you'd love a job with little responsibility, but after a few days on the job you were bored to tears.

One of the next decisions to be made is location of your potential employment. A woman might be trained in a specific profession, but if she lives in a small farm community where that type of work just isn't available, she has a serious decision to make. What would be best: to uproot her children at this tumultuous time in their lives and move to a larger city, or to take a less-challenging and less-paying job where she is?

If she decides to move, she will have the emotional burden of reassuring her children that they will make new friends, in addition to arranging for new living accommodations.

Sometimes a woman is tied to a low-paying position because she doesn't have the finances to be able to move to an area where she could obtain a high-paying job. This is a tragic plight in which many women find themselves locked.

Women who are able to obtain jobs which provide the same salaries as married men experience less prejudice against their marital status. No one realizes this more clearly than the woman with children who must support her family on inadequate welfare payments.

In her book, *The Woman Alone,* Pat O'Brien states, "She is acutely aware that a public-aid check in her mailbox means exclusion from the society of 'normal' hardworking Americans who see her as something useless. Our necessities are legally defined as her luxuries. For example, 'You tell me to shop with food stamps and not buy soap,' challenges a welfare mother. 'But I'm supposed to be clean and my children are supposed to be clean. How do I handle that?' "

Another problem faced by women returning to the business world is outdated or inadequate education. With the information explosion, knowledge becomes outdated almost before it is assimilated.

Many women are limited in the job market because they are unable to afford school or training before returning to work.

College enrollments have increased extensively in recent years due to the many women returning to school. Many, of course, are married women who want to finish their education and obtain their degree because their children are now in school or grown.

Many others, however, are newly divorced girls who have set their goals for positions which require further education or who have set their sights on salaries which require more degrees.

Some divorced women are even willing to take the risk and sell their house to finance their education.

Funding is often available to women, especially those with children to support. I know of many women who were able to obtain scholarships or at least loans so they could get their degrees.

Sometimes it may be necessary to take a temporary job while enrolling in "plug-in" refresher courses. And even if a woman already has the necessary degrees, attending evening school at a local college can be marvelously enlightening.

It is amazing how returning to college can quickly orient an over-30 woman to what's happening in the world. College students can be fantastically helpful in mirroring your outdated ideas, and attending college can give you an added confidence and boost to your ego. The innovative courses now available at most colleges can open up exciting worlds previously unknown to many women.

I enrolled in a filmmaking course which was challenging and fun. I'll probably never be a professional filmmaker, but I can take some good footage when necessary. Not only was it a satisfying experience, but at the same time it became a family project. My kids and I worked on my homework — filming a canoe race or driving into different locales and filming cultural life-styles.

I also met many other divorced persons while attending evening school. Conversation over a cup of coffee and a piece of pie after class was often as educational as the class itself.

However, a college education is not always necessary for a creative, challenging career. Don't ever assume that any position is out of reach because your experience or education is limited. If you demonstrate enough initiative and enthusiasm, many employers are open-minded about hiring persons with little education. Some prefer experience to education and are willing to train a talented beginner.

Dr. Theodore Newcomb, professor of psychology at the University of Michigan and author of numerous works on education, recently pointed out: "Most things college students learn they forget quickly. In the main, they come and go through college and remain basically the same people as when it all began."

Here and there, you will find employers who have experienced the results Dr. Newcomb talks about.

These are the open-minded employers who put a lot of value on other abilities and talents as well as amount of education or experience.

You may have to survive many interviews and long days of waiting for replies before the right job turns up. Expect to never hear from a large percentage of the companies where you've sent resumes.

The securing of a meaningful job solves, at least partly, the financial problem, although child care often takes a large chunk of a paycheck when there are preschoolers or young school-age children. But a working mother has new problems. Sometimes baby-sitters turn out to be unreliable, or your children react negatively to their methods of discipline.

Some preschoolers fit right into nursery school. Others resent it and fight against going. A mother who has to drop off a crying child each day and continue on to her job has a lot of mental juggling to do. She has to handle her sympathetic feelings for her child and get them out of the way in order to be professional and efficient by the time she arrives on the job.

Many churches have accepted the challenge of providing preschool day care. Almost always, the children receive such love and special attention at these sessions that some of the guilt and pressure is taken off the mother as well.

Here are some tips for evaluating a day-care center. First, set up an interview and then talk with the director and teacher. Observe carefully the children attending. Then take into consideration:

1. maximum capacity of the center
2. any income restrictions

3. age group of children served
4. financial aid available
5. a good racial and ethnic mix of children and staff
6. volunteers
7. work experience of staff
8. basic method of discipline
9. responsiveness of staff to children and parents
10. attractiveness of rooms; if projects are displayed
11. whether parents are invited to meetings and welcome to visit in classroom

Naturally, your final decision regarding day care will be influenced by cost, programing, and the availability of transportation, as well as food and napping facilities.

Your location might make finding a reliable mother-substitute especially difficult. My children and I live in a school district where even though we live eight-tenths of a mile from the school, the children are not allowed to eat lunch at school. It was costing me a considerable amount of money to find a baby-sitter who was willing to sacrifice every lunch hour. The pay had to make it worthwhile for her to miss out on luncheons, etc.

Eventually, as an answer to prayer, I felt the best move was to put my children in a Lutheran school. While I now pay tuition as well as a bus fee, the special attention as well as the spiritual training they receive are well worth the money. It is about the same amount that I paid for a baby-sitter the previous year. Here they eat at school and ride the bus each way.

A number of the seven million single mothers in the United States decided to organize, and they founded a group called MOMMA, consisting of single mothers. The purpose was to build a community of women who can talk to each other without having to explain themselves. They contend that single mothers are subject to discrimination and pressures by shocked parents, landlords, employers and credit agencies.

They believe that their organizing reduces the isolation and frustration that many feel in raising children without the help and companionship of a mate.

In addition to the usual challenges involved in child-rearing, MOMMA points out the additional dilemmas single mothers face: how to divide their time between their own needs and their children's, how to handle family authority, how to help children adjust to a "weekend daddy," etc.

To help solve some of these problems, MOMMA has become involved in projects working with child-raising and day-care facilities.

One interesting plan MOMMA is involved with is called co-parenting, in which divorced couples are helped to work out joint custody or mutual parenting of their children.

A monthly newspaper, also called MOMMA, is published by some members. (Mailing address is found in the list of helpful organizations at the back of the book.)

Some mothers have found that their jobs eventually give them self-confidence and a sense of accomplishment which have, in turn, made them more interesting and objective mothers. When a mother becomes less worried and more financially secure, she passes this confidence on to her children.

In addition, a mother who works tends to install more of a sense of responsibility in children. She usually assigns them more chores to complete. The time the family spends together becomes more valuable — the emphasis is on quality rather than quantity.

Working mothers simply don't have time to smother their children!

# 4

# Weekend Fathers

LONELINESS CAN BE a terrible companion. It can encourage a normal, mature person to make decisions he will long regret. Loneliness is more common to a divorced man, because usually it is he who moves away from the familiar home setting and family routine. Memories of happy times with his ex-wife and children can be especially painful to a man who is in a strange setting with considerable time alone.

One of the most obvious dangers is that a newly divorced person will be so lonely that his "bad marriage" doesn't seem as bad anymore. It is easier to remember the good times when you are lonely and forget why the divorce came about in the first place. There is a tendency, in fact, to idealize your former mate and to forget completely his undesirable characteristics.

In his book, *Creative Divorce,* counselor Mel Krantzler told of his own experiences in beginning life as a single man again. He described his small apartment with paper-thin walls and smelly, drab furnishings. The bed was uncomfortable and the young man downstairs was always playing the drums. And Krantzler detested housekeeping. His buttons were always missing, and he never managed to get to the laundromat before the last pair of socks was in the hamper. His cooking was lousy. (He admits he sounded like a male chauvinist at this point.)

When he first had occasion to return to his large comfortable home on a suburban street in a quiet section of San Francisco, he stated, "I felt a surge of nostalgia for the 'good old days,' and I panicked. *What* good old days? This wasn't what I was supposed to be feeling. I had said good-bye to all that, hadn't I? I had consciously chosen a different way of living. Had I made a mistake?"

As he walked up the steps to the house, he thought about the past three weeks of his life. The lonely evenings, the one-night stands, all those dirty dishes. "Maybe we could try it again," he thought. "Maybe we have 'learned our lesson'; maybe the separation jolted us enough so that we can discover new joys in our marriage."

He goes on to say that he realized later that he was going through the painful but necessary act of reconfirming that the relationship was over emotionally as well as legally. He writes, "I could see that returning to the old relationship was impossible, but what did I have to replace it?"

Because his new "home" was unbearably lonely, he had started a pattern of eating out, then going to a movie, and finally ending up at a bar. He eventually discovered that bars can be lonely places full of lonely people. Although his newfound freedom gave him a chance to meet a variety of women and supposedly enjoy the swinging bachelor life, he says that he did not enjoy it. In fact, he felt almost compelled to go out on the town and meet women, as though trying to prove he was not a reject!

After a while, he decided to stop feeling sorry for himself and to redirect his energies. He rented an unfurnished apartment in a better part of the city. It was larger, quieter, and newly painted, waiting for him to furnish as he wanted. He was surprised to find that he found furnishing and decorating it a challenge, and he enjoyed rummaging through furniture stores and garage sales.

With the apartment in order, he also felt a desire to keep the place clean. Managing his food and laundry no longer defeated him. He started sewing on his own buttons, accepting these tasks as necessary to comfortable living and not daily reminders that he was an abandoned husband and a worthless person. Soon thereafter he also began to make friends with himself again and found he enjoyed coming home to his apartment. He contacted some old friends and made new ones. As he says, "I was learning to separate out living alone from living lonely."

A man working out the emotions following a divorce often has difficulty releasing his deep-seated expressions and feelings. He often believes it unmasculine to simply cry, and the repression can be destructive to his system. A woman, on the other hand, is expected to cry, and her tears can be instrumental in restoring her to a healthier mental condition.

The problem of loneliness is usually worse when there are children involved. To the father usually falls the responsibility of telling his children the truth: he is leaving home and from now on will be living apart from his children and their mother.

It is very important that he reassures his children that he still loves them and intends to continue to see them regularly. He must be careful not to brush aside their questions but answer them honestly and simply. He must never make any promises he may be unable to keep. For example, to promise to see his children every Saturday might become impossible. He may have to tend to his own problems (moving, etc.) or work on Saturdays, especially in the early times of separation and divorce.

Maintaining communication with your children is essential. If distance isn't a factor, regular phone conversations can mean a lot.

If you can't phone, keep in touch by mail. In fact, a carefully written letter can be especially comforting and reassuring when the child is feeling lonely or abandoned. Encourage your child to write back. If possible, set up regular letter-writing days when your child sits down at a specific time and writes a letter about his day-to-day life.

Even today, though the tide is changing, the majority of divorce courts place children with their mother (approximately 90 percent are awarded to mothers), thereby putting fathers in the predicament of being a weekend parent. The supper table can be very lonely without your youngsters, and knowing that you are missing out on school activities can be painful. (It may be possible for both divorced parents to attend school functions from time to time. But many psychologists do not recommend this, since it usually arouses hopes for a reconciliation in the child's mind.)

A father suffering strong guilt feelings because he was the one who initiated the divorce often has a tendency to overcompensate by giving his children too many material things — more, in fact, than they really need or want.

A weekend father runs up against the problem of what to do with the kids. Most likely, his apartment is small and not terribly appealing to children. So they go the usual rounds: museums, parks, movies, zoos and sport events. The children end up overtired and the dad feels as if he is trying to buy their affection and outdo their mother. And while he and his children may have spent many hours together, he really didn't have an opportunity to communicate with his children, to learn what was new in their lives, and how they were feeling inside.

Weekend visitations can play havoc with a child's regular church attendance. One Sunday he may attend church and Sunday school with Mom. Next Sunday, with Dad. If the parents have been active in the same church, one parent may stop attending church altogether. On other weekends Dad may take the kids out of town, skipping church.

Most fathers are not aware of the tremendous influence they have on their child's spiritual understanding.

In *Your God Is Too Small*, J. B. Phillips writes:

A child's early conception of God is almost invariably founded upon the child's idea of his father. If he is lucky enough to have a good father, this is all to the good, provided of course that the conception of God grows with the rest of the personality. But, if the child is afraid (or, worse still, afraid and feeling guilty because he *is* afraid) of his own father, the chances are that his Father in Heaven will appear to him a fearful Being. Again if he is lucky, he will outgrow this conception, and indeed differentiate between his early "fearful" idea and his later mature conception. But many are not able to outgrow the sense of guilt and fear, and in adult years are still obsessed with it, although it has actually nothing to do with their real relationship with the living God. It is nothing more than a parental hangover.

When a father moves out of his home because of an unhappy marriage, he must be very certain that his children do not feel abandoned! Such a fear could indeed carry over into their understanding of God; they might believe that He, too, has abandoned them.

A Christian father still has a responsibility to his children to give spiritual guidance and be an example. When the father leaves the spiritual nurturing to the mother, it gives the children the impression that going to church and praying are not manly. Dr. Spock has stated that most children get their impression of God from their father.

The traditional arrangement of mothers receiving custody of the children has frequently proved unsatisfactory, according to Robert Goldscheider in "Not Only on Sunday" in *Parents' Magazine*. He writes:

It has led to frustration and bitterness on the part of fathers; to a sense of estrangement from their father on the children's part; and to a feeling of being overburdened practically, emotionally, and often financially, on the part of the mother. The separation agreements that provide such visiting rights are generally negotiated when husbands and wives are bitter and angry with each other. But whatever the marital conflict, and whatever the true grounds for the couple's separation and divorce — however irresponsible or cruel each may have been to the other — none of this necessarily implies that either is not fit to be a full and responsible parent. Nor does it imply that the best interests of the children can be served by custody arrangements and visitation rights which are not equally accepted by both parents. (In any case, such arrangements usually break down after a while, when children develop their own interests and want to share things with both parents.)

This author states emphatically, from his own experience, that "unless one parent is clearly disqualified, both should play a significant role in guiding the development of their children. Moreover, if the children are aware of their parents' joint involvement, some of the unsettling effects of divorce can be mitigated."

Since more fathers are becoming interested in obtaining custody of their children and because many mothers are interested in pursuing a career, obstacles to such arrangements are gradually decreasing. More courts are willing and even enthusiastic about considering unique arrangements for child custody.

A similar situation involves a young minister who has custody of his preschool son. His former wife wanted to return to college, and they both agreed that their young son would benefit from the male influence of his father. The minister discussed the situation with his congregation and, happily, they accepted and supported his decision.

An increasingly common but very difficult situation is when a mother abandons her husband and children. Statistics for runaway wives and mothers are staggering. The children then need their father's immediate reassurance, which is very difficult for him under such an emotional crisis. Since most fathers work for their living, they also have to make immediate arrangements for child care. But it is important, nevertheless, that no one put down the mother or try to break down the children's belief in their mother's natural love.

For most men, divorce is a financial blow. Economically, a divorced man usually ends up trying to support two households: his own and the home where his former wife and his children reside. This usually puts pressure on him to put in extra hours at work. This can, of course, also limit his own social life.

To some men, divorce can be a release of many unwanted responsibilities around the house. The man who arrived home tired each evening to have his wife greet him at the door with a list of urgent repairs may find his empty apartment a relief. Those men who felt "married" to their home, having to always keep the lawn just right, add the newest extras, etc., might find for the first time in their lives that they can pursue hobbies and enjoy outdoor recreation.

On the other hand, a man who loved remodeling and fixing up his home and took great pride in it, will find a void in his life, especially if he and his wife shared an interest in decorating, antiquing, gardening, etc. He may feel that he has really lost all his side interests in the deal. An apartment can be very confining to a man who previously enjoyed outdoor work and had a large lawn to care for.

All these problems and situations require the emotional healing of time and friends. Even after divorce, professional counseling can be very important, especially for single parents. The quicker a divorced parent can adjust to the divorce, the more support he is able to give his children. Feelings must be talked out, not held in. This may be especially difficult for a man who feels that showing emotion is unmanly. If a professional counselor or pastor isn't available, he should seek out trusted friends or other divorced men and women.

# 5

# Children of Divorce

SITTING ON OUR WINDOWSILL, drinking in sunlight, is a healthy, very much alive plant. It was given to my children last Easter by the Sunday school department of our church. It is symbolic of the new life in Christ we all can experience through Christ's resurrection. We, too, can come forth in newness of life.

In my mind, this plant also symbolizes the new life, vitality and potential of our family. For years, my children brought home plants every Easter, and every year the plants died very soon after arriving in our home. They simply did not seem to be able to survive in the environment our home provided. It depressed me to see the plants wither and die, but nothing I did kept them alive.

Until now! This is the longest any of our plants have stayed alive — and certainly this is the first one to last past Christmas. It is green, full and has numerous new buds, very symbolic of a healthy life.

Plants actively respond to their surroundings and can actually wither and die when in an unhappy environment. How much greater an impact does an unhealthy atmosphere have on children? Children also react in a dramatic and real way to their environment!

Most psychologists agree that what a child experiences and learns during his first six years of life determines largely his attitudes and habit patterns throughout his lifetime.

Dr. Fitzhugh Dodson, in *How to Parent,* says, "Your child's self-concept begins as soon as he is born." He goes on to say, "The most important thing your baby acquires during infancy in *his basic outlook on life.* He is forming, from a baby's point of view, his philosophy of life; his basic feelings about what it means to be alive. He is developing either a basic sense of trust and happiness about life, or one of distrust and unhappiness. Whether your infant will develop a sense of trust or distrust is determined by the environment you provide for him."

Dr. Dodson also brings out the fact that it is at this young age that a child develops either a basically optimistic self-concept or a pessimistic self-concept, which will continue in later life.

Awesome statements, these, making it impossible to ignore the fact that a child cannot live in an unhappy home without being affected by it to one degree or another.

Each year, between three and four hundred thousand American children are involved with the experience of divorce. However, studies have brought out a very important fact regarding children from broken homes. J. Louise Despert, a medical doctor who is author of *Children of Divorce,* states:

> We have been told repeatedly that divorce is a major cause of juvenile delinquency. Yet a study of approximately 18,000 delinquent children by M. C. Elmer revealed that *only one-tenth of delinquent boys and about one-fifth of delinquent girls came from families broken by actual separation and divorce.* From what kind of homes, then, did nine-tenths of these unhappy boys and four-fifths of these unhappy girls come?
>
> Not, we may be sure, from well-adjusted families in which both parents were on the job . . . the largest proportion of these children who fall foul of the law come from families which are emotionally broken, *without* having their disharmony overtly recognized by a recourse to law.

These facts and many others enforce my conviction that sticking with a bad marriage for the children's sake is usually the worst possible reason for two adults to live together. Yet, especially among the Christian community, it is common to hear people say, "They should stay together, if only for the children's sake."

Is it really better for children to live in such destructive environments? Homes characterized by anger, frustration, stress and hurt can't possibly give children an optimistic and healthy self-concept. Often, in addition, a child believes he is in some way responsible for his parents' unhappiness, and this further destroys his self-image.

Dr. Despert gives a loud "no" as she continues:

While the physical separation of parents brings many urgent problems in its wake, it is not the severest blow to children. The emotional separation of parents from each other, and of parents from children, works its destruction on children in homes where the word divorce may never have been breathed.

With actual divorce we are likely to find the situation opened to the light of day. Parents who have arrived at a decision to divorce must also decide what is to be done about their children. For many parents, this is the first time that they become aware of their children's difficulties. It is the time in many cases when they turn to the minister, the doctor, or a clinic or psychiatrist for help.

Divorce also often brings the child's buried anxieties to the surface. The divorce has not created these anxieties. They have been there throughout the period of dissension. They may have been born long before. The remoteness between parents is usually accompanied by a parallel emotional remoteness between the parents and their children.

Another researcher who backs up this premise is

Morton M. Hunt, author of *The World of the Formerly Married*. In his book he emphatically states:

> The treasured folk belief, *children hold marriages together,* is inaccurate. In fact, the more acceptable divorce becomes to Americans as a solution to marital difficulties, the less force children exert in keeping marriages intact. People used to feel that they should endure their miseries and stay together for the sake of the children; today they are giving ever greater weight to their own right to happiness, or perhaps coming to think that it is no favor to children to maintain an unhappy marriage for their benefit.

Finally, Dr. George R. Bach, co-author of *The Intimate Enemy* and founder and director of the Institute of Group Psychotherapy, concludes:

> Once a marriage is clearly sick and unsalvageable, divorce is the best way to assure the sanity of the partners and, especially, of children. Youngsters are infinitely better off in a clear-cut divorce situation than in a subtly crazy-making family.

> Within homes, children are likely to become strategic weapons of adult warfare, and very few parents have the slightest idea of the resulting psychological havoc.

> Some children exist for years, hearing their parents

viciously arguing, but scared half to death that they might actually separate and divorce. Finally, when the parents do break up, the kids usually discover that, in reality, their lives have improved. Things got better, not worse. The very thing they were so afraid of wasn't as bad as the time spent in dreading it.

Certainly I am not encouraging every couple who has family squabbles to get a divorce! Seek out counseling, yes; divorce should never be taken lightly.

There are many cases of seemingly hopeless marriages where the couple mutually decided to commit the situation to the Lord and then worked hard at making the marriage work. After patient waiting and diligent prayer, often there were marvelous results. No one can satisfactorily explain why in some cases marriages are almost miraculously healed and in other cases, even after fervent, sincere prayer, things don't work. Does it have something to do with the *mutual* prayers and efforts of the marriage partners?

Since my divorce, I have seen a great deal of improvement in my own children's emotional stability.

When my daughter, Pam, was in third grade, her teacher and the principal asked her father and me to come in for a conference. (We were still unhappily married at the time.)

They said Pam was showing signs of becoming emotionally disturbed. Immediately Pam's father became defensive and said angrily, "There is nothing wrong with her. She is just a normal eight-year-old."

Although he was against it at first, we did receive counseling from a family service organization recommended by her school. However, they made us face up to reality when they said, "You are not going to solve your daughter's problem until you solve your own marital problems. Her condition is the result of living in the home situation you are providing."

*"We don't have a problem,"* my husband insisted. And I'm really not sure, even today, if he believes there was a problem.

I have tried very hard since my divorce to provide a stable home for my children. Often I've failed completely. When I am over-tired, my nerves become frazzled and I become edgy and cross. I also painfully remember how, shortly after my divorce, I went through a temporary stage when I was just so tired of trying to provide a nice home I almost gave up. Luckily, friends nudged me and helped me see how I was going to hurt my children. They risked causing me to be hurt or angry and pointed out that my children needed certain routines, regular mealtimes, etc. I knew they were right, and I soon snapped out of that rut. My friends had stuck with me through all my problems, and I couldn't let them down and disappoint them.

People who have known Pam since she was very young often tell me when they see her now, "My, Pam has changed. She is so much more cheerful and outgoing. She seems so happy and secure." Of course, Pam still has her own problems and difficulties, but these improvements have been very reassuring.

In her junior year of high school, Pam took a course called Child Development. As part of the initial introduction, her instructor asked each class member to give a brief oral resume of himself, especially stressing his own family life and growing-up period. Then, each class member passed around a piece of paper to his classmates with only his name on it. Each classmate was asked to write a one-sentence statement about each other member of the class, based on the information that the students had shared.

When Pam brought her paper home to show me, I was thrilled. On it were many positive comments, with only two on the negative side. The ones that encouraged me the most were, "Your family really loves you," and "Your relationship with your mom sounds great," and "You seem like such a happy person." These words from her peers were valuable to me. They also were another encouragement that I was on the right track.

Dr. Paul Popenoe, founder and chairman of the board of trustees of the American Institute of Family Relations, stated: "Sound family life is the largest factor in mental health, broadly speaking. Apart from definite genetic conditions, the early upbringing of children, centered largely on the atmosphere of the home, is more significant than any other single influence in determining whether an individual will be able to develop mental and emotional normality, be able to relate usefully to other persons, marry successfully and produce children who, in turn, grow up with good mental health and make a constructive contribution to the work of the world."

Atmosphere in a home is not necessarily determined by the presence of two parents in a family. It can be created by a single parent who wants "home" to be everything the word implies.

In *The Family Fun Book,* authors Helen and Larry Eisenberg say: "What does a family need most? In a changing world, the family members need an anchor. A deep religious faith is a part of that security and another important part is the role of the family — a small group of folk who can be counted upon. In a world on the move, every individual needs to feel: 'I count. My family love me. Though all others fail me, my family will not.'"

My kids and I are *family.* Each member has his own interests and responsibilities. We come together at night as a unit, close the doors to the rest of the world, and comfort and enjoy each other in the way only a family can.

If you have children, you will discover that along with the other changes brought about in your life because of divorce, you have also received a new title: single parent. This status brings on a number of new responsibilities and problems at a time when you are under considerable emotional upheaval yourself.

There will be many decisions to be made regarding your child and his everyday routine. How will custody arrangements be worked out? Will it be necessary to obtain day-care services? Will your child have to move or change schools? How will you handle dual loyalties?

Both you and your child are undergoing a period of change; and a traumatic change is never easy, no matter what your age. Children often feel especially helpless! Sometimes they are not told what is going on and only know what they have overheard from bits and pieces of conversations. This adds to their anxieties.

It is important to prepare your child for this adjustment as much ahead of time as possible. Even though he most likely is aware of a strain at home, he may not be expecting a separation. If he is old enough, there are many excellent books available. A good example is *The Boys' and Girls' Book About Divorce* by Richard Gardner.

Understanding the emotional needs of your child and finding ways of meeting them is essential. A child can absorb and survive almost any painful experience if he is certain of his family's love. Take extra time to reassure him that nothing has changed regarding your love for him. If you can successfully convince him of that fact, he will be better armed to face any comments from friends or neighbors regarding the family breakup.

I believe it is unfair to place a child in the position of being asked to choose which parent he would prefer to live with. On the other hand, it is a good idea to sit down and discuss how he feels about the changes in his life. Does he have a particularly strong feeling about which parent he will be living with? Take seriously the questions he asks and try very hard to look at the divorce from his young eyes. How does he really feel?

Both you and your child are struggling through the painful experience of adjusting to the loss of the family unit. Try to help your child release the special hurts within by letting him pour out his emotions to you. It is natural for a child to experience a variety of emotions, such as hostility, guilt and grief.

At a time like this, the demands on a parent are considerable. Understanding the strain your child is under and expecting certain difficulties can help you be patient and objective.

Most divorced parents feel a sense of guilt and this makes it even more difficult to be objective. Self-accusation and guilt are universal emotions experienced by almost every single parent. If necessary, seek help through your minister, counselor or any social agency (see list of helpful organizations at back of book) to help you express and work out these deep-seated feelings. Otherwise these feelings can cause tensions between your children and yourself. And nothing should be allowed to cause friction between parents and children who are struggling with the changes brought on by divorce.

Many children believe that the parent who has left home has abandoned them. Sometimes a child becomes hostile to the parent he blames for the marital breakup. The older the child gets, the more he may have almost an obsession to make one parent the "guilty party" so he can fix the blame on the parent and relieve himself of unfounded guilt.

Sometimes a child believes he is to blame for his parents' separation because of just one isolated incident. He may feel, for example, that, "Daddy left home because I was screaming. He said he can't stand my screaming."

When children express their fears and feelings in this way, it can be very painful to the parent. Basically, each child is very afraid of being left alone and uncared for. If one parent left, he reasons, what guarantee do I have that this one won't either?

A child may seek out a friend or relative to whom he will pour out his troubles. This can be very therapeutic, if the person he selects is careful not to offer biased advice. The painful emotions must be released, but certainly not intensified.

A girl often becomes hostile toward her mother; she may believe that her mother wasn't a good enough wife to make her dad happy, or feel that her mother sent her dad away. This can cause a mother to feel that she has let her daughter down, and, in fact, failed as an example for her.

Yet, it is often very common for a young child to be very close to his mother, but then as he reaches his middle years, become less dependent on her and prefer his dad's company. A girl may be less open about it but may feel this way also.

Parents can relieve pressure on their children by talking things over, asking how the divorce makes the child feel, and above all, admitting mistakes and shortcomings.

Likely, too, the children recall vividly some of the arguments which took place shortly before the parents separated. Words said in anger between parents may haunt the child and be blown out of proportion in his mind. Talking it over may help clear the air.

Whenever possible, it is preferable to protect the image of the absent parent. It can only hurt your child to put down his other parent. There is far more benefit in casually pointing out positive qualities.

Children sometimes put a parent into a situation of having to defend himself at the expense of the other parent. For example, a child may complain to the parent he does not live with, of how much work he must do at home. The parent should resist the temptation to say, "Why, that's terrible. A boy like you needs time for fun, too," and instead mildly allow the child to release resentments without actually feeding them or taking the child's side.

A child usually becomes very uncomfortable if he senses one parent trying to get him to take sides. Yet, he himself, in an unconscious effort to punish both his parents, may instigate trouble and try to start arguments between parents. If the parents are already angry with each other, this is often easily executed.

Parents must work very hard at remaining objective and neutral in such sticky situations.

Divorced parents sometimes transmit to their children unhappy feelings about marriage. These are all situations which mature parents can talk over and clarify in their child's mind if they take the time to do so.

Be careful not to be overprotective because of the divorce. Becoming too concerned about your child's activities and friends can cause new problems. Every child needs the opportunity to be creative and to experiment with certain ideas. He learns by facing problems, especially in relationships with his peers.

On the other hand, many divorced parents make demands on their children which are too extreme. I don't believe it is fair, for example, to tell a second-grade boy, "You are the man of the house now and must help your mother." He is not a man and does not deserve such an enormous burden. Of course, he should be assigned certain responsibilities and be expected to carry them out.

Be careful not to fall into the trap of reminding your child on every possible occasion of how much you are sacrificing for him. Naturally it is overwhelming for a divorced mother to have full responsibility for her children, but it isn't fair to transfer that pressure onto her child. Then he will feel guilty because his mother has to work so hard for him.

Earlier in this chapter I deliberately took time and space to list many encouraging statements about children who are from broken families.

While ideally the best thing you can do for your child is to provide a happy home, becoming discouraged or disillusioned can't possibly help your child. The statistics are encouraging. Many single parents have successfully raised lovely, stable children.

One of the most meaningful steps I have taken in helping my own children was providing good male adult models for them. For a number of years, my son was surrounded by women: myself, my teenage daughter, his teacher and the various baby-sitters. Eventually I was able to make arrangements through the Evangelical Child Welfare Agency in our community to set up sessions with a young male counselor. In my daughter's case, she was fortunate in being assigned a very sensitive, concerned counselor at her high school. In addition, she is active in a Young Life Club which is led by a person-centered Christian man who has taken an interest in Pam.

There are many excellent books dealing with the particular problems which sometimes arise among children from broken homes. Excessive closeness of mothers to sons, or fathers to daughters can become exaggerated in single-parent situations and lead to future sexual difficulties. Studies confirm that adolescent girls who have grown up without fathers or adequate male-role models often display inappropriate patterns of behavior in relating to males. Preschool boys raised without fathers tend to be more feminine. In other cases, young boys develop extreme masculine behavior as they compensate for the absent father.

Professional advice from Christian psychologists or counselors can be essential. Usually they operate on a scale according to income, and are well worth the money spent.

For quite a while a national car rental agency, which was second largest, had a slogan, "We're No. 2, and so we try harder." Although that has negative connotations, it is also a very positive statement. I believe that, because I realize the problems inherent in raising a child in a broken home, I must admit it is second best. But, then, I, too, try harder!

# 6

# Sticks and Stones

*Sticks and stones may break my bones,*
*But names will never hurt me.*

THAT'S NOT TRUE! Stone-throwing and name-calling do hurt — very deeply. And while words may not be able to physically kill someone or break bones, they can cause deep emotional scars, bring feelings of inadequacy, and totally destroy a person's self-confidence. They also can delay indefinitely the healing processes so necessary for total recovery from any traumatic experience. Moral and religious judgments indelibly imprinted on a divorced person's mind also can cause deep guilt pangs.

Though it is estimated that one out of every three and a half marriages in this country eventually breaks up, the traditionally minded element of society still often imposes upon divorced persons the feeling of being a second-rate citizen. *Nice people don't get divorced.* It is something to be ashamed of — something irresponsible.

Unfortunately, Christians are often the chief stone-flingers. Even though the Bible clearly warns against judging the faults of others, we Christians are almost eager to criticize others and jump to conclusions without knowing half the facts. We think of ourselves as super-detectives discovering every last sin (of omission or commission) of our neighbor, all the while ignoring our own. The unknown poet advised us well when he said: "Don't be too harsh with the man who fails — or cast at him a stone — unless you are sure, yes, very sure, that you have no faults of your own."

The Bible warns us over and over about judging the faults and failure of others. Jesus certainly made His position clear when a woman caught in adultery was brought before Him. The Pharisees seemed to derive pleasure from pointing out that Mosaic Law commanded such a woman to be stoned to death. (They also were hoping to trick Jesus.) But Jesus replied, "Whichever one of you has committed no sin may throw the first stone at her." Slowly everyone left. Jesus then said to the woman, "Is there no one left to condemn you?"

When she replied, "No one, sir," Jesus said, "I do not condemn you either. You may leave, but do not sin again" (Jn. 8: 1-11, TEV).

Jesus put great personal worth on each individual. He spent a great deal of time making sure people realized their self-value, and worked hard rehabilitating them. Over and over He made it clear that God cares deeply and personally for every human being. Yet, many people cannot personally apply the compassion Jesus showed for people. Mentally they find it hard to believe that Jesus loves them. But it is God's love for each of us that reassures us of our own personal worth.

After a divorce, no one feels very secure. Even the person initiating the divorce, surprisingly, usually ends up feeling worthless and rejected. Divorce causes the same feelings of remorse and insecurity in both sexes; it is a failure; a blow to the ego.

But there is a positive side. In rising to the crisis and developing new ways to handle rough situations, a divorced person can grow and develop into a more fulfilled, more mature person because of the experience of divorce. Being able to face squarely those who hint that you are a failure can be a strengthening experience in itself.

Statistics tell us that one out of every nine adult Americans has been through a divorce; the divorced person is certainly not alone. And these men and women are not misfits, but normal, average people whose marriages ended.

Divorce should not be a form of punishment. It is merely the process of burying a dead marriage and recognizing and rejoicing over the rebirth of an independent single person. It should not be considered tragic. The person locked into a destructive, unhappy marriage without any hope for release is the person to feel sorry for.

Divorce is a second chance — an opportunity to discover oneself again, to set new goals and to start living all over again. It can be a reawakening experience, the beginning of a meaningful new existence.

The first step in the healing process, preparing the way for readjustment and happiness, is the reaffirmation of the divorced person as a worthwhile, valuable human being. At the time of divorce, many people feel inadequate and believe they just can't make it on their own. The whole situation seems overwhelming.

But they survive. And with survival comes the realization, "Well, I got through it. I didn't think I could, but I did. I'm stronger than I thought and actually have accomplished quite a bit." The more we increase our ability to function well, the more our feelings of failure and helplessness decrease.

The first year after divorce can be a crucial one. It is very important that feelings of loneliness, depression and failure are dealt with. The longer they are kept inside, the longer the delay will be before the divorced person can experience a release from guilt and fear and loneliness. Ignoring these feelings or keeping them hidden only increases their intensity.

Many people (especially men) often feel they cannot expose their deepest emotions. They feel this is not an acceptable way to express them. But feelings and emotions which are unexpressed and therefore go unconfronted do not disappear despite their invisible character. Instead, they are transformed into tension and anxiety which take their toll on the body. Ulcers, tension, headaches and overeating are common examples of inability to deal with day-to-day emotions. Hostility that is not expressed directly usually comes out indirectly, quietly hurting the people around you. As people notice the effect of stress and tension on their bodies they have begun to look for ways to release the tension, emotionally and physically.

A positive aspect of the women's liberation movement has been a concern that both men and women be allowed to express the full spectrum of emotions. Many divorced persons are tormented by guilt feelings and unable either to forgive themselves or accept God's forgiveness. Mentally they may realize God's willingness to forgive them, but spiritually they feel too unworthy to either ask for or accept that forgiveness.

Since society has a tendency to put high demands on the woman's role as wife and mother, women are particularly susceptible to feelings of guilt and failure at this time. These feelings stem from unrealistically high demands which society has placed on them.

The Gospel speaks to us where we are, whatever our predicament. We need only to believe it and turn ourselves over to God for His rehabilitating work. If this is a special problem for an individual, how important it is that he receives guidance from either a pastor or a lay witness. This is a predicament no man needs to be locked into, because God Himself has provided the release and relief.

Often, too, severe feelings of hostility and bitterness toward the ex-mate can destroy a divorced person's self-image. Praying for the former mate and asking God's forgiveness for both of you can help so much. Ask God for power to forgive your former spouse of any injustices against you, and He will not ignore your request.

I wasn't aware of how much hostility I was harboring toward my former husband. However, I later realized how resentful I really was. For one thing, I resented the fact that I was weary and over-tired from working and caring for our three children while it seemed that he was busy enjoying life without nearly as many responsibilities. Of course I realize now that he wasn't enjoying life as much as it looked like at the time. But I did not realize how much energy I was wasting by resenting him. Then a friend in a prayer circle wrote a letter to me one day. She said that she felt the Lord had directed her to write and point out to me that I had all these hostilities and resentments seething within me, below the surface. I was sure I didn't, of course, but decided to pray about them, just in case! I also took her advice to pray silently whenever it was necessary for me to be with my former husband. (Whenever he was picking up the children, especially.) I can't express the difference that made in my attitude toward him.

I could tell that I wasn't nearly as sarcastic or easily offended or defensive. Of course, I still occasionally resort to a bit of resentment, but usually only when I have neglected to pray about the situation.

Frequently a divorced person is so over-critical of himself that he becomes a victim of "personality abuse." He must be made to recognize what he is doing to himself so he can begin to develop a more optimistic viewpoint. He must resolve to stop dragging up the past and to start living in the present.

Self-criticism is increased when people make comments such as, "Are you sure you didn't give up too easily? Did you do *everything* possible to save your marriage?" You begin debating again within yourself whether there were things you could have done differently.

The divorced person must realize and accept the fact that any rejection by others is not personal rejection, but rather a rejection of divorce. People often convey a dislike of a divorced person when it is actually the condition of divorce they may dislike. Often, too, an accusing person is a very unhappy person himself, one who doesn't have the stamina or strength to break out of a bad situation. Consequently, he is unconsciously envious of the status of the divorced person and in defense has to make moralistic judgments. Understanding *why* people put down others helps a divorced person handle such rejections maturely. It may be that the divorced person can, by being aware, be of help to the accuser!

During the first year or so, it can be especially helpful to seek out other divorced persons and build friendships with them. They are the persons who will understand you best and have the most constructive advice to offer. There are a variety of groups for divorced persons, some more helpful than others. (See the list of helpful organizations at the back of the book.) Take the risk of reaching out for new friends. Divorced persons are often the most understanding friends in the world. They know what it is like to go through the emotional, spiritual and intellectual dilemma of divorce and are usually very sensitive to other people's needs.

Small groups (not necessarily singles) can also be

very helpful at this time. Hopefully, most churches have sharing groups where the community of believers unite in small gatherings to encourage and listen to the needs of each other. There also are many other types of therapeutic groups, such as transactional analysis, sensitivity groups and Faith at Work forums. It helps to realize that other people have felt the very same way as you. They have experienced similar misgivings and fears. You soon discover that most of your feelings are very normal under the circumstances.

Through groups or individuals, you can begin to regain your self-respect and self-image. Then comes the best part. As you begin to recognize in yourself those self-defeating habits, you can replace them with more appropriate behavior.

You see, for example, how self-pity can actually prevent you from really stepping out and enjoying life again. Naturally, in the first months after their divorce, most people are somewhat overdependent on their friends. This is to be expected, and, in fact, is helpful. But, if, after a period of time, the divorced person does not begin to become independent, the friends may well begin to feel a sense of obligation and possibly a bit of resentment. They feel they *must* invite the divorced person over regularly or *must* include him in every plan. This feeling of obligation can work on divorced persons as well, but in a different way. They begin to feel very obligated to their friends for all the free meals, etc., yet they wonder how they can ever be valuable enough for their friends to put up with their dependence. They worry about how they'll ever be able to repay all these people for their kindness.

The very fact that divorce releases you from the hostilities often experienced near the end of a marriage can also give you new incentive. You begin to like yourself again and find that you have many valuable qualities. Within the confines of your past marriage, possibly only part of your total person was exposed. Now, other aspects of your personality can be discovered and cultivated.

A person returning to a single status has to learn all over to talk in the singular tense. No longer is it, "We love to do that, or this," but *"I* enjoy. . . ." The newly single person must learn to think positively about this status. Too often the marital status of a person has too great an effect on his self-image. Some persons find a certain amount of self-esteem in their marriage; for example, this is especially true of a woman married to a man of high status in the community. This woman might be extremely personable, capable and creative in her own right, but she has fallen into the habit of relying on her husband's title for her own significance as a person. Losing this crutch at a time when she is already depressed can be especially devastating to her, although it obviously should not be.

Many people returning to a single status feel incomplete because they still see themselves as only half a pair, and the other half is missing.

Asserting oneself and developing a new self-image can have fantastic results, both on the individual as well as on those around him. Being around a person who is sure of himself, without being egotistical, of course, is a delight to others and attracts new friends. But a person wallowing in self-pity or existing with a low personal image tends to drive people away. Developing this new self-image may take some time and many mental gymnastics, but we all have an inner need to be, as Marlo Thomas says, *"free to be me."*

Now that a divorced person is again living as a single, she can create her own new life, making it what she wants. As transactional analysis prescribes: "Write yourself a great new script."

You are on your own now; there is no marriage partner to try to please, or to blame, or to depend on. This is an opportunity that not everyone has to start over and rediscover yourself. Make the most of it. Set some time aside to sit down and think over what you want to do with the rest of your life. Set goals; some immediate, many far-reaching. As the posters declare: "Today is the first day of the rest of your life."

# 7

# What Do the Scriptures Say?

WHEN JESUS HAD FINISHED talking on these matters, he left Galilee and went on to the district of Judea on the far side of the Jordan. Vast crowds followed him, and he cured them there.

Then the Pharisees arrived with a test-question.

"Is it right," they asked, "for a man to divorce his wife on any grounds whatever?"

"Haven't you read," he answered, "that the one who created them from the beginning made them male and female and said: 'For this cause shall a man leave his father and mother, and shall cleave to his wife; and the twain shall become one flesh'? So they are no longer two separate people but one. No man therefore must separate what God has joined together."

"Then why," they retorted, "did Moses command us to give a written divorce-notice and dismiss the woman?"

"It was because you knew so little of the meaning of love that Moses allowed you to divorce your wives! But that was not the original principle. I tell you that anyone who divorces his wife on any grounds except her unfaithfulness, and marries some other woman, commits adultery."

His disciples said to him, "If that is a man's position with his wife, it is not worth getting married!"

"It is not everybody who can live up to this," replied Jesus, "— only those who have a special gift. For some are incapable of marriage from birth, some are made incapable by the action of men, and some have made themselves so for the sake of the kingdom of Heaven. Let the man who can accept what I have said accept it" (Mt. 19: 1-12, Phillips).

As a Christian, the most difficult problem for me by far in deciding upon divorce as my course of action, was facing directly the Scriptural viewpoint and Biblical statements on divorce. For many years the words of Jesus in Matthew 19 kept me from seriously considering divorce as the most logical solution to my problems.

Those words seemed to indicate to me that divorce was not the way for me to go; yet, I'd ask myself over and over, "What *is* right? Is it right for my children and me to stay in a home that is destructive and unstable? Does God really want my children to spend their formative years, when they are so impressionable and vulnerable, in this setting?"

Finally I realized that, for me, the key to this dilemma was my understanding of God. As a Lutheran, I had studied the catechism well and the words, "We should so fear and love God," had been deeply imbedded in my heart and mind. So I knew well that we can't underplay obedience to God's laws.

However, I finally asked myself, "Why *did* God give us laws to live by?" Was it because He was rigid and demanding? I decided — and still believe — it was because He knew best what would give us the greatest overall happiness and make our lives the most meaningful they can be.

Therefore, His rules about divorce were meant to impress strongly on us His wonderful design *for* marriage. As described in the Bible, marriage was to be a relationship of fulfillment, planned to bring joy and love and respect. God intended marriage to represent on earth the image of the union between Christ and His Church characterized by devotion and self-sacrifice. God chose marriage as the means through which to perpetuate the human race. So it is understandable that Jesus also tried to reinstate in people's thinking the original plan of God for marriage.

Even though I decided, after much prayer and serious thought, that divorce *was* the direction God was leading me, I was, for a while, still uneasy whenever I was confronted with Jesus' words (Mt. 19: 1-12). Even so, as I look back today over these past six divorced years, there is no doubt in my mind that, while divorce is certainly not God's perfect will, for me to get a divorce *was* right. He has not for one moment deserted me and my children. In fact, I have been definitely conscious of His presence in our daily lives.

During these years, I have gained some insights about the Scriptural viewpoint of divorce which I think might help others. In writing this chapter, I have prayed sincerely that God will so guide my words that I do not put down in black and white any ideas or words which might direct anyone to go against God's guidance in his own life. I have not intended to recommend taking Jesus' words lightly or looking for loopholes. I believe one thing very firmly: each person must make this spiritual decision for himself or herself. It is a decision you will have to live with. It must be right for you, and only you can make it.

I think we must keep in mind the total context of the situation Jesus was in when He talked about divorce. We need to know the attitudes of the people living then. We also need to consider our own attitudes and the cultural influences that brought us to our particular viewpoint.

Divorce and the variety of positions on it in the Christian community are not new. Though the divorce rate is reaching an all-time high now, throughout history there have been marriages that were in trouble or that ended in divorce.

In *Barnes' Notes on the New Testament*, it says, "At the time (during Jesus' life) the people were very much divided on the subject. A part said that a man might divorce his wife for any offence or any dislike he might have of her. Others maintained that divorce was unlawful, except in the case of adultery."

Christians today are equally divided on the subject. On the one hand are those who believe it is better for couples to get divorced than live in hostility and unhappiness. And it really doesn't seem to be in line with God's will that people be so desperately unhappy! On the other side are those Christians who state firmly that divorce is unbiblical. They are right, too.

Most Christians today probably believe there are some situations when divorce might be justified. But then the debate begins over which situations warrant it.

And that is just the very trick question posed by the Pharisees. They were well aware that they were dealing with a very controversial subject, and they hoped to get Jesus into a disagreement with His followers.

R. Lofton Hudson, in *'Til Divorce Do Us Part,* says:

Jesus was accustomed to using strong, brief, unqualified assertions to drive home unfamiliar and unwelcomed truths, like if your hand offends you, cut it off, or if your eye offends you, pluck it out.

He hated the way authorities were quibbling over the details of how to get rid of a woman and be justified. So he put men and women squarely on the same basis, though not quite committing himself on the woman's right to divorce her husband — no more than he attacked polygamy or slavery. He said simply that such ruses used by the men in that culture overlook the original goals of marriage. This we can all agree on.

Women today are shocked at the way the Jewish laws worked against the rights of women. The injustices of providing no way for a woman to end a marriage had just become recognized. In fact, ways for a woman to force her husband to divorce her were being considered. However, Rabbi Hillel, an influential religious authority, interpreted the Law so liberally that he permitted Hebrew men to divorce their wives for every trivial complaint. The cultural tradition put women in much the same category as a parcel of land or a donkey; she was her husband's property to do with as he pleased. (Since having children was so important to their tradition, many Hebrew men divorced their wives because they couldn't have children.)

Divorce for these women was very bad. What

could they do? They might go back to their parents' home or they could become prostitutes. There were no provisions at that time for women to earn a living! So Jesus was protecting women from economic helplessness.

(Hudson points out, incidentally, that Jesus never really said, "until death shall you part" or "as long as you both shall live." These statements were the products of the marriage ceremonies developed in the Middle Ages.)

But more important, Jesus referred them to the original design of marriage. Albert Barnes in *Barnes' Notes on the New Testament* says:

> Jesus called their attention to the original design of marriage — to the authority of Moses — an authority acknowledged by both parties.

> The original intention was that a man should have but one wife and should bind himself more strongly to his wife than to his father or mother. The marriage connection is the most tender and endearing of all human relationships: more tender than even that which unites us to a parent.

> The word "cleave" denotes a union of the firmest kind. It is, in the original, taken from "gluing" and means so firmly to adhere together that nothing can separate them.

> The argument of Jesus here is that since they are so intimately united as to be one, and since

in the beginning God made but one woman from one man, it follows that they cannot be separated but by the authority of God.

Jesus admitted that Moses allowed divorces but still contends that this was not the original design of marriage. It was on account of the hardness of their hearts Moses founded the custom in use. He did not deem it prudent to forbid a practice so universal; but it might be regulated and instead of suffering the husband to divorce his wife in a passion, he required him, in order that he might take time to consider the matter, and thus make it probable that divorces would be less frequent, to give her a writing; to sit down deliberately, to look at the matter, and probably also to bring the case before some scribe or learned man, to write a divorce in the legal form. Thus doing, there might be an opportunity for the matter to be reconciled and the man to be persuaded not to divorce his wife. This, says Jesus, was a permission growing out of a particular state of things, and designed to remedy a prevailing evil. But at first it was not so.

The disciples were full of Jewish notions. They thought that the privilege of divorcing a wife when there was a quarrelsome disposition or anything else that rendered the marriage unhappy, was a great privilege and that in such cases to be always bound to live with a wife was

a great calamity. They said, therefore, that if
such was the case—such the condition on which
men married — it was better not to marry."

As a woman, I cannot help but react to the lack
of simple respect and consideration these men showed
the women of their time.

I am afraid that we are so eager to find rules that
we do not really hear what Jesus said. He said, "No
man therefore must separate what God has joined
together." Does this apply, then, to the couple who
got married with one, or both, ignoring or taking
lightly the total commitment in marriage to God and
to each other? Can we really assume that God has
joined them? Or is it, really, legal adultery? No matter how hard one marriage partner may try to make
God the Head of the house, if the other spouse is
not willing to allow God to direct and guide the marriage, the order which God sets up for marriage falls
apart.

And when Jesus says, "It was because you knew
so little of the meaning of love that Moses allowed
you to divorce your wives!" I really relate to that.

When I got married, I don't believe I really understood the deep meaning of love. If I had, I do not
believe I would have entered into marriage without
first being certain that my husband accepted Christ
as the Authority in our marriage and was willing to
commit our marriage to Him. So many couples think
they understand love, and later realize that it was
infatuation, or a deep need to be wanted, etc. What
a difference when a marriage is dedicated to Him,

and entered into by two people who deeply love each other in a true Christian way.

But I am so grateful that God is loving and forgiving and has continued to bless us even when we make such serious mistakes as entering into a wrong marriage, or misunderstanding His guidance. I do not believe that God ever deliberately puts us in undesirable situations just to teach us a lesson. We do a pretty good job of getting into bad situations all by ourselves, usually because we haven't consulted Him first. But even when we do miss His best (or His will for us), He doesn't desert us but remains as our strength and guides us wherever we are; this is the New Testament blessing — God is love!

# 8

# The Church and Divorce

AFTER I'D BEEN DIVORCED about two years, a woman's magazine editor wrote to me and asked if I'd write an article on the subject of "Being a Friend to Divorced Persons." As I prepared the article, I realized all over again how very fortunate I'd been because I had been loved, supported and encouraged over and over again by the members of my church. They were there when I needed them, whether my need was physical, mental or spiritual.

I remembered how shocked and disappointed I had been when I first discovered that not all persons getting a divorce had experienced this kind of love. It was painful to hear of their experiences. Many had actually been hurt deeply by Christians who either ignored or judged them.

What a contrast my experiences were to that of a girl I met in a media class. Over coffee one evening after classes she told me bitterly how critical the members of her church had been when she left her husband. Her eyes flashed as she said, "Well, I don't need those phonies or their lousy church. I can find more honest, down-to-earth people in a bar than in that church. They think of people as numbers — to make their membership list impressive. But if you don't live your life according to their rules, then they don't want you around."

I tried to convince her that not all Christians were like that. But her mind was closed. She said she'd had enough of church people to last her a lifetime, and then she changed the subject abruptly.

Wow! How different her experiences were from that of one woman who had had five bad marriages! This woman, in fact, had decided to simply live with the next man in her life since marriage did not seem to work for her.

How was she treated? Well, the Bible tells us that Jesus felt she was worth His concern. He met her where she was — at the point of her need — and got down to what was really her most urgent need. He cared for her as a person — as a woman!

I have run into a few closed minds myself, at various times, but not from the members of my church. So the few experiences I have had did not disillusion me about God or His Church.

Probably the most painful experience I had was at a Bible camp one summer during family week. A pastor who was on the program discovered that I was divorced. He had run into my former husband and listened to his side of the story. Without even asking to hear my side, or thinking about the behavior patterns of alcoholics, he approached me after breakfast one morning.

"You realize you are being very stubborn at your family's expense, don't you?" he said.

At first I thought he was kidding me about something — last night's volleyball game or wiener roast, maybe. But a second glance told me he was perfectly serious.

"I don't know what you are talking about," I said.

"You weren't thinking about your children when you got a divorce," he continued, "just yourself and your own wants."

I burst into tears as I cried, "How can you presume to understand my situation? You've just met me!"

My angry outburst and tears simply convinced him that I was full of guilt feelings. The rest of the family week was considerably strained for both of us. Luckily for me, the camp director, also a pastor, was fully aware of my situation and was able to calm me down and help me be more objective.

Now, after a few more years have passed, I realize that I became overdefensive. If a similar situation should come up in the future, I believe I will be able to handle it calmly and without such an excessive display of emotion. But, I have often wondered, what if I hadn't experienced the love of Christ through my Christian friends and my own pastor before running into this man? Would his efforts at "instant counseling" have turned me away from the church and disillusioned me? How many other people have experienced similar confrontations by pastors and church members?

There was a time when the pastor was just about the last man a couple considering divorce would go to for help. Because, at one time, most ministers, like the one just mentioned, felt that they had to do everything in their power to keep a marriage together, no matter what. A couple with marital problems usually knew that and would avoid adding a minister's disapproval to their confusion. But times have changed. Fortunately, most modern ministers are very sensitive to the problems of the members of their congregation. A minister may even be aware of the couple's difficulties and offer his services before the couple contacts him. Many pastors are even wise enough to ask the couple, "Have you considered divorce as a solution?" This is certainly not his recommendation; but by his recognizing it as a possibility, he frees the couple to be completely honest with him without fearing his disapproval.

It is encouraging to discover that individual ministers of all denominations are getting special education in order to be better trained to help persons going through the trauma of a difficult marriage or a subsequent divorce. They are aware that an understanding of the use of modern psychology can be very helpful and are eager to apply the principles of human behavior to their congregation.

The American Psychiatric Association in their newsletter, "Psychiatry-at-Work," reported that a panel of ministers and psychiatrists met to discuss ways in which the special knowledge of each could be helpful in the other's work. This would be especially effective in counseling divorced persons since many divorced persons have contact with both a pastor and a counselor.

The pastor and the members of his congregation can be supports to couples with marital problems as well as in assisting newly divorced persons make the necessary adjustments.

A couple seriously considering divorce has everything to gain and nothing to lose by first getting professional help. If their pastor feels he is unable to give them the type of help necessary, he can refer them to a psychologist, psychiatrist or professional marriage counselor.

Professional counseling may enable a couple to work out their personal problems and save their marriage. Some couples cannot afford to spend money (or at least believe they can't afford it) on a counselor. They are willing to talk things over with their pastor, however.

A judge who presides over many divorce suits was quoted in a newspaper as saying that, in his opinion, 85 percent of the couples who appear before him could have made a go of their marriage if they had wholeheartedly wanted to. He felt this kind of desire was not likely to arise where there is a readiness to resort to divorce quickly.

Many couples are, on the other hand, establishing the practice of going to a counselor each year for marriage checkups.

This is all the more reason for ministers to get as much education as possible in marriage counseling.

John Vayhinger, in the book *Before Divorce*, states two reasons why he believes marriages today are under such stress: either the partners showed such terribly poor judgment in courtship that they selected mates to whom they could not relate, or they found suitable mates but could not carry through the learning tasks of adjustment necessary to make the relationship rewarding and satisfying. With the passage of time, disappointments and disillusionments replaced early hopes and dreams. A pastor or marriage counselor who intelligently and sensitively relates to the couple may help them understand why they were unable to make the difficult adjustment necessary to a satisfying marriage, and to make the necessary changes.

Estimates have been made through various research studies that approximately 60 to 65 percent of couples seeking help are able to resolve their conflicts.

Pastors expect that more than two-thirds of their counseling will deal with family conflicts between husbands and wives or children and parents.

Some of the most common problems of couples considering divorce are:

1. *Constant arguing and venting hostilities on each other.* Some marriages exist on the fight and make-up method. This tears down the self-respect of both parties, and the question they must face is, "Do the good times outweigh the bad?"
2. *One major blowup which has caused seemingly irreparable hurt.*

3. *Marital infidelity.* While this is grounds for divorce, it need not be. If it is a case of one affair and the mate is now sorry and realizes the mistake, the question is whether the other mate can handle and accept the revived love.

4. *Imagined infidelity and/or excessive possessiveness.* A good marriage should allow for human behavior. A wife should be able to have lunch with a business or personal friend, openly and honestly, and vice versa.

5. *One mate has matured and outgrown the other mate, who has regressed.*

6. *Sexual problems between the marriage partners.*

7. *Financial difficulties.*

8. *Communication difficulties.*

Dr. Anthony Florio, author of *Two to Get Ready,* believes that many of the couples who enter his office with troubled marriages should never have been married in the first place. He said they are like patients who see a medical doctor with an advanced case of cancer. They are coming for help, expecting too much too late. So it seems obvious that an important role of the church and clergy should be to help prevent divorces by effective premarital counseling.

Statisticians estimate that one million persons are thinking about getting a divorce this year and already have made an initial contact with their lawyer. Approximately 587,000 will withdraw their case and not go through with it. At any rate, all these persons will need the support and affirmation of others, and what better vehicle of support is there than the Christian church? Quite a mission for every Christian.

The pastor and members of a congregation can be especially helpful in assisting a newly divorced person to make the necessary adjustments. The divorced person has conflicts, guilt feelings and loneliness which can all be worked through the help of concerned Christians. I believe one of the most meaningful services a church can render to divorced persons is to convince them of Christ's saving grace and love so they can accept His forgiveness for mistakes made and then forgive themselves.

There are so many ways that the members of a congregation can be helpful, especially to single parents. To begin with, they can help when the family moves, invite them to dinners, offer rides to special meetings and programs and just give warm fellowship and acceptance. Invitations to a father-son or mother-daughter banquet when a divorced parent is unable to attend, and offers to baby-sit so a divorced parent can have some time to herself are other suggestions. But, at all times, be sure that these acts are carried out with the idea of them being of mutual benefit. Avoid making a divorced parent feel like you are trying to be useful and he happens to be your "cause."

Katie Wiebe writing on the subject "Can a Widow Survive in Today's Church?" says:

> Unfortunately, our churches do their share in perpetuating a couple-dominated society.
>
> Friends sometimes wonder why I hesitate to

attend church suppers and banquets. It is simply because I don't enjoy being sifted out of the crowd to sit at the table with the people who don't fit into the coupled society.

At one large supper gathering I found myself and my children and another husbandless woman ushered to the children's table. I dismissed the matter as inconsequential. When on another occasion the incident repeated itself, I began to understand that some people think a widow doesn't really count as an adult.

At another large banquet a lady friend and I agreed to go together. As we entered the banquet hall, the ushers asked us if we would mind splitting up and taking single seats which they found difficult to fill with couples. I wondered later how many *married* couples had been asked to do the same?

What then can the church do? Certainly not isolate singles but utilize the full potential of single people. Offer less sympathy and more actual acceptance.

Of course, the author of the above article is not saying there isn't a place for single parents or any newly divorced or widowed persons to meet together as groups. Churches can be very helpful if they are able to arrange various sessions or retreats for these adults, preferably including persons from other churches or working with other congregations to provide such groups.

Many churches have been effective in ministering

to divorced persons by including them in "sharing" groups of transactional analysis groups ("I'm okay. You're okay").

Our Bible camp director was especially concerned about the number of formerly married adults who came to camp. So he arranged for a retreat weekend for these persons, inviting a pastor who was active in social service ministries to conduct the sessions.

Being a Christian and being divorced can be a complicated situation in other ways. Because you are involved in many aspects of the Christian community, you find yourself in a rather unique situation. Many Christians do not believe you can be both a Christian and divorced. And many well-known evangelists and other Christian spokesmen can be successful in making you feel like the man without a country: you don't fit really well in the Christian community (at times) and yet, you as a Christian do not feel that the secular community is where you choose to be.

As youth director of my church, I often took a group of teenagers to Jesus rallies and other similar activities. One speaker I was anxious to hear was David Wilkerson, and I still admire and respect him tremendously. But he makes such a point of speaking out against divorce that in doing so he does a good job of making already divorced persons feel like outcasts.

Then one day I happened to hear a talk show with Bob Harrington (Chaplain of Bourbon Street). He also had some things to say about divorce and seemed obviously prejudiced against women when he made the statement, "There is a Delilah trying to get into every man's pocket, and that's why there is so much infidelity these days." I wished I could have phoned him and said a few things in behalf of women, but I chalked it up to the same kind of male chauvinism that I've run into too often in the Christian community.

I know of a case where a young woman, who became a Christian after being divorced, tried to enroll at a Bible college. They made a big issue over her having been divorced and finally ordered her to bring her divorce decree to their office so they could see for themselves on what grounds it was issued. They wanted to be certain she was the "innocent" party! When she appeared with her preschooler in tow, they proceeded to give her second-degree treatment and make her feel like a third-rate person.

For years I have quoted an old saying, "The church is not a hotel for saints, but a hospital for sinners." And I believe that includes every one of us.

Another area in which Christians disagree in regard to divorced persons concerns encouraging divorced Christians to accept offices in the congregation. I've previously mentioned that my church hired me as a youth director, but I've also heard of situations in other congregations where the members weren't as forgiving. I can understand their point to a certain extent. They are sometimes afraid that the church may come under reproach if they have divorced persons as church officers. They are probably sincere in their fear of bringing dishonor to Christ's name.

It is difficult for me to comprehend how anyone

who studies Jesus' methods of dealing with people and His attitude toward sinners can believe it is Christian to force divorced persons to take a lesser place in the community of believers.

One writer compared the enthusiastic forgiveness often given to a repentant convict to the judgmental put-down sometimes given a divorced person.

I've also read about a dedicated couple who became Christians after each had been divorced and they had been married. They left a congregation they loved because they were told he could not be given a position on the church board.

The subject of remarriage brings up still more differences of opinion among denominations.

Even today there are many Christians who are extremely opposed to remarriage. In fact, some pastors go so far as to believe that persons who have remarried should break up that relationship. They point out that since Jesus said, "Whosoever shall put away his wife and marry another committeth adultery," persons who are married for a second time because of divorce are continuing in adultery.

In an article in *Evangelical Visitor* entitled "Divorce and Remarriage: Is It God's Permissive Will?" author Dwight Replogle recommends the separation of remarried persons. He states, "Isn't it just plain common sense that since remarriage is adultery and adultery is sin, that the sinning must stop if the one involved is to remain clear before God?"

He firmly advises other pastors to follow his suggestions: "What if those advocating acceptance of remarriage are wrong and Christ meant exactly what

He said when He called remarriage adultery? O Lord, just help us! Think first, of all we have told that remarriage was all right, and they are lost. Then think of our own souls as we stand before the judgment bar of God and hear God pronounce an awful indictment against us for going our own way. We may have a retort now but we will be speechless then! O Lord, I would rather be safe than sorry, rather be safe than lost. God help us to see the danger of our deliberations and the consequences."

I would have liked to ask this author how he would have handled remarriages where the couple had children as a result of the union.

Some pastors find themselves in precarious positions when it comes to their willingness to perform remarriage ceremonies. There is a definite inconsistency in the practice of many denominations that will not allow their ministers to perform ceremonies for divorced persons entering into a second marriage. Yet many of these same denominations will enthusiastically welcome these divorced persons and add them to their membership rolls as long as a minister from another denomination has officiated at the remarriage.

I was thrilled when a friend asked me to be her attendant at her second marriage. But I was disappointed to discover that she planned to be married by a judge since she didn't know any minister who would marry them. For many years I had told her about my church and invited her to visit us. I had also told her what a concerned person my pastor is. So it was very exciting for me to be able to say, "I am sure, if you both go and talk with my pastor and discuss your situation, that he will marry you."

He did, and it was a meaningful service. Her parents were very pleased and I was grateful to my pastor. Otherwise they might have entered into this very important relationship without the benefit of a Christian ceremony and Christian counseling.

# 9

# Rocky Ledges

DIVORCE IS EXPENSIVE, both emotionally and financially. Legal procedures are costly and complicated. They intensify animosity and often even invite perjury. The present legal system serves best those who can afford the fees and neglects those who cannot. Middle-income persons are usually most financially pressed.

On the one hand, the middle-income wage earner does not qualify for the legal aid of either the publicly or privately funded agencies which set very low-income eligibility standards. On the other hand, private legal fees are often prohibitive. The problem is most acute in civil cases, where the rule of court-appointed representation does not always apply, and even more so in domestic relations cases which provide the most numerous contacts the average citizen has with the legal processes.

Except for the wealthy, divorce usually involves a reduction in the standard of living for both individuals. However, most couples believe that not even this can make it worth enduring an unhappy situation.

Occasionally divorce becomes unnecessarily expensive, when one or both of the parties are so anxious to obtain freedom that they make decisions about property division, child custody, support and other financial situations without thinking them through objectively. Because of their emotional level at the time, their value judgments become distorted.

A woman may be at a distinct disadvantage if, during the time she was married, her husband handled all the finances, including insurance coverage and annuities, interest and taxes, stocks, bonds and dividends, etc. She may find herself unknowledgeable about making financial decisions and even budgeting her money. For example, statisticians have estimated that most widows spend at least 80 percent of their lump insurance money within one year after receiving it. For these and other reasons, it is important, whenever possible, to obtain sound legal counsel recommended by a reliable source. With effort, arrangements can be made so that legal matters can be worked out with a minimum of stress and a maximum of mutual cooperation.

Each state has its own list of legal methods to end a marriage. The first step in the legal maze of obtaining a divorce is usually to find out the state's eligibility requirements. It is *not* necessary to obtain a legal separation before beginning divorce proceedings. In some jurisdictions it *is* necessary to be separated from a spouse 30 days before filing for a divorce. (This regulation can be waived if one spouse has been physically and cruelly abusive to the other and/or to the children.)

The *fault system* of divorce, where one has to prove that a spouse did something horrible to the other and/or their children, is an extension of the advocacy system of the law, where two lawyers fight it out in court. This benefits no one and can do much harm.

Legislation has been initiated in many states and passed in some for the no-fault divorce system. California was the first state in the nation to pass this system.

Shortly thereafter, various companies came out with do-it-yourself divorce kits costing from $5 to $25. Instead of spending up to $400 for an uncontested split, most of which would be paid to a lawyer for filling out and filing the forms, with the kit couples needed only to fill out the forms themselves, pay a $20 court filing fee, and show up in court 20 days later.

The Maricopa County (Arizona) Superior Court clerk's office estimated that do-it-yourself filings made up about 20 percent of all dissolution filings within the first year after they became available.

Problems can arise when one party is out of state or doesn't agree with the dissolution. One judge, who hears an average of 30 do-it-yourself cases a week, commented that too often the husband and wife have not settled between themselves property divisions, child custody and support. If they have neglected this he must insist that they get a lawyer. Many lawyers believe it is being penny-wise and pound-foolish when couples skimp on something this important while they spend money freely on luxuries and entertainment.

Men and women do not always receive equal treatment under present divorce laws. Every year divorce reform bills have been introduced into state legislatures, but usually they are shelved or defeated. In Massachusetts, for example, there has not been a significant change in divorce laws for over 100 years.

In most cases, credible witnesses must be provided to corroborate the testimony. (There are occasional cases where no witnesses are necessary to corroborate the testimony of a party.) One of the most difficult tasks of a person seriously contemplating divorce is to request friends to be his witnesses at the divorce hearing. It took me quite a while to get up the nerve to ask my friends to appear at court with me.

One couple had been my strong supporters through the shaky, traumatic years of my marriage. They were well aware of the problems which had been tearing my marriage to shreds, and had been the best possible friends to my husband and me. They certainly didn't enjoy the idea of getting up in court and speaking out against my husband in my defense. But, as they said, "It is one thing to hand out advice and another thing to stand up for what you've said and carry it out. But, of course, we will do it."

And they made my day in court far less painful. They picked me up at my job, took me out to lunch and prayed with me on the way to the courthouse.

Grounds for divorce differ in various states. However, the following situations are most common across the nation. The most widely used ground for divorce is cruel and abusive treatment (also called mental cruelty). The next most commonly used ground is desertion. A husband must have left without consent and in some states be gone for two consecutive years before a wife can file for divorce on grounds of desertion.

Interestingly, few divorces are granted on grounds of adultery, though Biblically this is the most acceptable ground. The reason for this is that since divorce records are public, the court is usually concerned about the effect this could have on the couple's children. Allegations of adultery must also be supported by other than circumstantial evidence.

Also, though excessive intoxication and use of drugs are often the cause for a divorce, the divorce is usually granted on the grounds of mental cruelty.

A man who has sufficient ability to support his spouse but grossly, wantonly or cruelly refuses to provide suitable maintenance or support, can be divorced on this ground. Termination of utilities and eviction notices are usually used as evidence.

The only time a spouse can obtain a divorce on the grounds of impotence is when proof can be provided of an incurable condition at the time of marriage. Neither infertility nor childlessness is sufficient evidence.

A spouse can divorce a mate who has been convicted of a felony.

Usually the action is filed in the county where both last lived together if the husband still resides there. Otherwise it may be filed in the county where either one presently resides, provided residency requirements of the particular district have been met.

Alimony can be requested only at the time of divorce, except for specific circumstances: for example, if the question of alimony was reserved at the time of the divorce or if there was no personal jurisdiction over the husband at the time of divorce. Some women feel alimony is an accrued income for years of child-rearing and husband-tending.

A woman can be at a severe professional disadvantage if she gave up a promising career to get married. The years in which she would have furthered her career were spent in the home. While her husband spent these years advancing in his career, she may be finding it necessary to start all over. In fact, she may have to attend classes to update her knowledge in her profession.

In the past, most women received alimony payments whether there were children involved or not. However, since women have become more active today in the professional world and more job opportunities are available to them, fewer divorces involve permanent alimony payments. Some experts estimate that about 85 percent of women in divorce actions *do not* receive alimony, and a few experts estimate as high as 95 percent. Sometimes alimony is paid in gross; or periodically for a short time.

However, women who cannot provide for themselves and their children must be supported whenever possible by their ex-husbands. This is required by state laws set up to insure that dependent members of a family do not unnecessarily become public wards. A husband's whereabouts and ability to pay are obvious considerations. Divorce laws, as previously stated, vary in each state, and some experts believe that laws favor a woman who is out to get what she can as compensation for having to become a divorcee. Alimony can turn into a lifetime penance.

Many state laws consider alimony as an award to the "innocent" party and thus a punishment for the "guilty" one, usually the man, according to Bernard Steinzor, author of *When Parents Divorce*. Consequently, he writes, many husbands are tempted to distort matters so they can sue their wives for divorce, since, if they are successful, they may not be liable for the wives' future support. Thus archaic divorce laws that insist that one party be the plaintiff and the other the defendant encourage battles over children and money. When alimony is considered as a fine levied on the guilty husband, the courts often will disregard the wife's assets in setting the amount.

Whether or not alimony payments are made is usually determined by taking into consideration the earning potential of the wife, the number and ages of the children, the wife's health and her standard of living during marriage.

Interesting recent developments which have been occurring as women have become more active in the employment field are cases where ex-husbands have felt their wives should pay them alimony since they were more secure financially.

127

Laws and courts cannot always be depended upon as deciding what is the best interest of the children. Since there are no statutory guidelines, judges have enormous discretionary power in deciding matters of paternal fitness and child custody, division of marital property and the assessment of support and alimony.

A judge, however qualified, makes his decisions based on his own background and a variety of experiences which influence his thinking. In some cases, the judge bases his decision on legal advantages, with little awareness of what is best for a child. Court calendars are often overcrowded, and even most judges will admit that the first case each day receives far more attention than the last. Therefore, a child's well-being can depend upon the alertness of a weary judge.

So, unfortunately, important decisions regarding child custody, support and visitation rights are often made during highly charged emotional outbursts when they should have been resolved as much as possible *before* the hearing.

Asking a child to select which parent he'd prefer to live with puts him in an unfair position unless he is a teenager. It is advantageous, however, to sit down and discuss with the children their feelings about their parents and the divorce. But if the child has to actually make the decision, he'll likely feel guilty toward and extremely sorry for the parent he did not select. This is a heavy burden for a youngster.

Sometimes lawyers can maneuver special privileges for their clients, but these privileges or advantages may not always be in the best interest of a child. When a parent is able to afford a lawyer with special contacts, that lawyer may use those advantages for the benefit of his client at the child's expense. Until recent years, in order for a father to obtain custody of his children it usually meant an ugly drama in the court and almost invariably put the mother in a position of scandal.

Michael McFadden, in his book *Bachelor Fatherhood,* points out that in the past, for a father to obtain custody he would have to prove his wife to be unfit, and she generally had to fall into one of five categories: (1) nymphomanic or sexually promiscuous while children were in the house; (2) an alcoholic; (3) a child-beater or grossly neglectful; (4) mentally incompetent; or (5) a lesbian.

The mother who did not fight back was assumed to be one (if not all) of the above. If she did contest, there was a sordid courtroom drama with neighbors and friends being called to take sides. Today trends are moving toward seeing the logic in a father raising his children, especially when his ex-wife plans to return to further her education and accept a position which would require a total change of lifestyle for the children. (See chapter 5.)

In some cases, payment of alimony and/or child support may be requested by the court in a final lump sum, as in the case of a man who may be a bad financial risk in the future but has money now.

According to a report by the U.S. Commission on the Status of Women, a survey in Wisconsin showed that one year after a divorce, 42 percent of the ex-husbands make no support payments at all and another 20 percent are in arrears. Finally, most men just quit or cut out and run.

Once a wife has filed for divorce and the action is pending, she can initiate procedures for temporary support and custody of children in addition to obtaining a restraining order, should that be necessary. The amount of the support payments is determined by the judge at the time of the hearing, based on the assets and income of both parents. Usually an amount is designated for each child. Care should be taken to discuss who pays for extras, such as medical expenses, summer camp, etc. The parties involved must be sure these are included on the divorce decree.

If the father has fallen behind or is deliberately not paying the court-ordered support, the mother can go back to court to enforce the order. A district court can issue a criminal support order and warrant for his arrest, or it can order a wage attachment or lien on any property he owns. However, the court will take into account any changes in the father's financial condition in assessing his responsibility.

Remarriage of the parent having custody does not generally affect child custody or support payments. The father must continue to support his children unless the second husband legally adopts them.

Stipulation also should be made in the divorce decree regarding who will get the tax-dependency exemption. Alimony payments are tax deductible from the ex-husband's income, and the woman must pay taxes on them. Child-support payments, however, are not considered taxable income. (A list must be kept of all expenses for the children, including school expenses, Y.M.C.A. or camp expenses, park district fees, etc., or a person's mind will go blank at income tax time.)

Various tax laws seem inconsistent. For example, the following is condensed from *Women's Yellow Pages* in an article entitled "Short-changed Again: Tax Deductions for Child Care."

January 1, 1972, Congress passed new tax benefits for those paying for child care. This new section No. 214 provides for increased deductions for child care and a new deduction for household service expenses.

The deductible amount is a maximum of $4,800 a year as compared with the old $600 for one child and $900 for two or more.

This deduction may only be used by persons who are gainfully employed and is, therefore, a work-related expenditure, designated as a personal living expense distinct from a business expense. It remains in the category of one of the many itemized deductions taxpayers can take in lieu of a standard deduction. This, in fact, creates a discriminatory situation. The average working family and certainly the working poor, those who need the benefits most, are effectively barred from using the deduction, as usually only those with higher incomes have enough deductions to warrant itemization. A review of the eligibility requirements clearly demonstrates the discriminatory nature of this deduction.

The taxpayers cannot have an adjusted gross income which exceeds $18,000 a year. In placing this limit on income, Congress has limited the number of people who can take the full $4,800 deduction.

Also, the law states that payment made to a relative for child care *cannot* be taken as a deduction. Although the majority of children taken care of by persons other than their mother are cared for by relatives, this stipulation in the law almost forces women to place their children with strangers.

In *The Woman Alone,* author Patricia O'Brien says:

> Until recently, single men and women were financially penalized for their single status by being required to pay higher taxes than married persons. Now, ironically, new tax laws made it cheaper to live 'in sin' and file separate returns from the same household than to get married. One couple promptly filed for divorce, declaring they would prefer living in sin to paying higher taxes. (Surely those legislators who concern themselves with the morals of the country will find a way to prevent a mass exodus from marriage for financial purposes?)

A woman head of household already has a more or less ambiguous position in society, regardless of the reason for a husband's absence from the home. However, a woman who has to go on welfare has her feelings of inadequacy compounded by her inability to provide financially for her children. Many women have no option but to go on welfare. Unprepared for the role of provider because they have no job skills, discriminated against in the few employment possibilities they might be able to handle, receiving no help from the father of their children and being unable to arrange and/or pay for child care puts them in a poor financial situation. Contrary to public opinion, few mothers on welfare are taking advantage of their situation and enjoying it.

Divorced women in America are severely limited in their ability to obtain credit. Yet almost six million families are headed by women. These women need access to credit as badly as any man. Yet the consequences of blind assumption (for no one needs a steady income more desperately than a woman alone with children to support) prevents her from making use of many opportunities she should be entitled to. National credit companies, ironically, have been reported to discriminate against divorced mothers, even though much of their advertising is aimed directly at the women's market. Insurance companies, too, often discriminate against divorced women.

Make a list of all the items which require your change of address and status. I made costly mistakes by not stopping to realize how things could become complicated simply because my status wasn't accurate on a form!

My first shock came after I had been working and managing my children alone for about a year and a half. My daughter fell off her bicycle and knocked out her two front teeth (permanent ones, of course). It happened on a Tuesday evening in summer, at almost 9 o'clock. When she came running to me, at first I couldn't even think what to do.

133

She was in pain and I was about to panic. Fortunately, a teenager who was baby-sitting next door came to our rescue. Her boyfriend's dad happened to be a dentist, and she phoned him. Although he was just leaving, he agreed to wait until we could get there. (Later, when my head cleared, I realized how fortunate we were because most dentists' offices were closed on the following day, Wednesday.)

After the discomfort and disappointment came the financial blow. I was sure I had read my hospitalization policy at work, and knew it included dental accidents. So the following morning I stepped into the personnel director's office to discuss a claim. To my astonishment, I discovered that I was not covered! At the time I was hired, a bookkeeper did not bother to double-check about my marital status and simply assumed because I had children that I was married. The policy was designated to cover children only when the hospitalization was for a head of household, and at this company only males had been assumed to be heads of households. This was a very costly lesson and, thereafter, whenever I changed jobs, I became very careful about how my policies read.

Yet, in spite of all my precautions, later I again found myself penalized because a bookkeeper switched my status. On a recent income tax W-2 form, I noticed I was listed as 2 (married). In checking with the bookkeeping department, I found that again, in spite of all my precautions, someone along the way simply thought that I had made a mistake and switched my status from 1 (single) to 2 (married). This meant that throughout the year the correct amount of income taxes had not been deducted from my paychecks. It also required some changes and confusion.

Another item I never thought too much about was my children's bank accounts. They had accounts in Wisconsin, and since I felt that they were safe there I did nothing about changing banks. However, their father happened to receive a yearly statement of interest and decided to request new bank books. He informed the bank that the old books were lost while actually I was keeping them in a safe-deposit box. Once when the children visited him, he allowed them to withdraw some money to spend on toys. This upset me since I did not approve of using savings account money so lightly. When my bank checked with the Wisconsin bank, we couldn't believe the casual attitude this small local bank had toward issuing new bank books. Anyone could have brought in two youngsters and claimed to have lost their books and been issued new ones!

I'm sure I will continue to make mistakes, often due to lack of knowledge or serious concern about certain situations. But there was one situation where I was falsely accused and I stood up for my rights.

After my daughter had false front teeth fitted, she later had a second problem. The roots of the stubs of the original teeth became abscessed, and she had to have considerably more dental work. By this time, the dentist who had helped us the night of her fall had moved downstate, and we found a local dentist. He cared for her on an emergency basis and then gave her weekly treatments. We had arranged a budget plan and tried to keep up as best as possible, after making a down payment of one-third of the total cost. After the appointments were taken care of, I called the dentist's office since I was under the impression there were to be a few more appointments. I was told that all the work was now complete and the final bill would be arriving shortly.

When I received the final itemization there was one expense listed as "false tooth — $65.00." I stopped by the office and talked with the receptionist, who agreed to check this out. Pam's two false teeth had each cost almost double that amount and had been fitted and made by the first dentist.

I received no reply and phoned again. An assistant also promised to check it out and get back to me. She never did, and I just didn't send any more payments.

Then one day I received a notice to appear in court because of not paying the dentist bill. I was overwhelmed; it was so ridiculous! I tried to stop by the dentist's office, but he was evidently out to a late lunch. When I finally reached him, after much effort, he said, clearly and plainly, "I don't believe you. I think you are lying! I am sure that if I have down that I put in a false tooth that I did so." Then he went on to mention the fact that he realized I was divorced, and he guessed I just wasn't willing to be responsible for my bills. That hurt more than the bill, of course.

So I decided to take my evidence (the bills from the previous dentist) and appear at court, assuming the judge would at least hear me. After I took a morning off of work, the judge refused to even look at my bills, etc., and set up a second court date. He stated that the dentist would have to appear, which meant I was being penalized a second time because it would necessitate more time off from work. I asked the judge to please reconsider since I didn't appreciate having to take so much time away from work on a charge that I could prove was wrong. The judge reacted by saying, "We get women like you all the time, lady, trying to get out of your obligations." In spite of all my intentions, I ended up with tears in my eyes, probably convincing the judge of my unstable emotional condition.

By this time my lawyer had moved out of state. I was ineligible for any kind of state legal aid because my salary was over the maximum; however, I couldn't afford to hire a new lawyer when I knew it was so unjust.

Then I decided to contact the local YWCA. They were very interested since they have a task force which tries to help women who are being discriminated against. They agreed to at least have someone from their office appear with me at court as a witness so that they could help me contest any unfair judgment. As it turned out, the evening prior to the second court date, the dentist's attorney phoned and offered to split the $65. Since that would prevent my having to take additional time away from work, I decided to accept the offer. However, many times since then I've wished I could have figured out a way to prove myself without having to pay a lawyer.

Looking back now, it is easy to see how many costly mistakes I've made. But, at the time, I was so involved with simply working and raising my children that I neglected to be as cautious and informed as I should have been. *Divorce is expensive!*

# 10

# Building a House on the Rock

BEING DIVORCED AND ON MY OWN has been a lesson in dependency on the Lord. For some reason, I am a slow learner when it comes to spiritual lessons. Time after time God gives me His love and power to help me through a crisis. Over and over again He answers my prayers. When I realize how very real He is and how actively involved He is in my life, I am overwhelmed. Confident that I will never forget the lessons learned and will always, from this moment on, depend completely on the Lord, I tell all my friends about His wonderful love.

Then, the very next time a problem arises, I I promptly do the thing I said I would never again do. I panic! The fact that God guided me through the last situation seems to slip my mind completely. This problem seems different! This one is overpowering, in fact. Not until I attempt to muddle my own way through it unsuccessfully do I remember to commit it to the Lord.

In chapter 3 about working mothers, I mentioned how God led me to my first position in the religious publishing field. Now, as I sit here at my typewriter and reflect on the five years since I've been single again, I can see very clearly how God continued to guide me, step by step, moment by moment, through the ups and downs. It is amazing how clear it all looks from this vantage point in time. Yet, while I was living through the situations, I rarely was that conscious of the long-range view.

Shortly after I started out on my own, I began writing down my prayer requests in a special notebook. Each morning, during my devotional time, before my children are awake, I make a daily prayer list. Many are general prayers requesting God's presence in our daily life. Others are more specific: requests for God to help particular friends, or to guide in specific incidents. Some are prayers of praise, thanking God for His involvement in my life and His daily help and comfort. But, whatever they are, I write them down daily and keep the notebooks in which they are written. From time to time, it is very encouraging to read back a few months or a few years and rejoice again at how beautifully God has worked out so many of the problems. In fact, sometimes He worked them out so smoothly that at the time I failed to really grasp the fact that these were answers to prayers. Not until I read the prayers specifically and follow the day-to-day results do I see the direction in which He was leading.

These prayer notebooks have become somewhat of a diary of my spiritual life and how God continues to teach His followers.

By scanning a few pages I can remember, for example, when I first received a review copy of the book, *The Hidden Disciplines,* by James Earl Massey, published by Warner Press. It wasn't a particularly appealing book (no artwork; heavy copy), but evidently God wanted me to read it and soon led me to the chapter on fasting. Now fasting is something I hadn't really given much thought to, much less felt inclined to experiment with. But evidently God was directing me toward a new step in my spiritual journey, because soon I felt a real desire to fast. It turned out to be a joyful experience, and one of preparation and anticipation for the various experiences which lay ahead. So I prayed and wrote in my notebook specific thoughts about which I needed God's direction. I also asked Him to be very real to me.

I found that often, on the days when I fasted, something out of the ordinary would come up. For example, the very first time I fasted I made it through the day up until suppertime. Temptation set in as I fixed supper for my children. I felt as though I was starving. Then the telephone rang. It was the Sunday school superintendent of my church. He asked if I would be interested in teaching the high school Bible class. Without any hesitation I answered yes. I felt sure that God had been encouraging me to accept this job. I believe that those high schoolers did realize how much I cared for them and how sincerely I wanted to help them understand about the Lord.

Another time I suddenly found myself out of work. By then, I was working as editor of a trade magazine for camp directors. Without much warning, the publisher discontinued publishing the magazine. As usual, I panicked. Then I fasted — not perhaps the most unselfish use of fasting — but I was confident I could count on God to direct me.

I started making attempts to find a new job. Then the director of our Bible camp invited my children and me to spend the following week at the senior citizens' camp. He said there were lots of little jobs I could help with, and the older folks usually enjoyed having youngsters around. I went, with no idea where my next job would be. I stayed at camp all week, having a ball, giving little thought to my employment. When I returned home, a letter was in my mailbox, requesting me to call for an interview. I was hired two days later as the editor of a regional magazine.

Perfect timing — as only God can arrange. If I hadn't left town for a week, I very likely might have accepted a different position, one I would have enjoyed far less. But God was working everything out according to His perfect timing because He had a particular lesson He wanted to teach me that week at camp.

During that week at the senior citizens' camp, one of the college-age counselors asked me if I had read *Prison to Praise* by Merlin Carothers. I quickly informed her that I didn't believe his ideas at all. My prejudice was based on the first two pages of his book, and I had closed my mind to anything else. But this counselor was so impressed with what the author was saying that I agreed to read the book and then give her my "qualified?" opinion.

That day it rained, cooperating with my promise to read the book. The counselor was returning to college the following evening, so I didn't have much time. Well, I read the book and still wasn't completely convinced. However, I decided not to knock it without trying it. So I prayed most of the evening according to the suggestions Carothers made. He recommends, as the Bible directs, that we praise and thank God for everything in our life, even those experiences which are really painful and even those people who really hurt us.

I started reviewing my life and went back in my prayers to situations in my childhood, and then worked up to the present. I thanked and praised the Lord for everything I could think of, even though I felt it kind of artificial to do so. But I was anxious to try the recommendations for myself.

Finally, I fell asleep, without feeling any particular emotion except maybe a bit of relief as a result of releasing so many unpleasant feelings before God.

The next day I went about my work as usual. Gradually, however, I began to feel happier and more peaceful than I had for quite a while. In fact, I couldn't keep from humming songs like "God Is So Good" and other campfire songs. Being at camp just increased this joyful feeling. However, I fully expected it to disappear when I returned to the reality of home and unemployment.

But the feeling stayed. The rest of that summer my theme song could have been "I Have the Joy

Down in My Heart," because I really did. And the words seemed to jump out of other songs. Like the words from the song, "Joy Is Like the Rain": "I saw Christ in wind and thunder, joy is tried by storm." I knew what those words meant and even made a banner with them on it. It was unbelievable to me that though I was broke and out of work, I was so happy. I discovered that it is sometimes in the storms of our life that we find out how real Christ is.

The Bible tells about a great storm that came upon some men crossing a lake in a small boat. The winds began to rise and great waves developed, which threatened to swamp them. The men were in real danger, and they knew it. They also knew where to find help. It happened that Jesus was napping in their boat. When they called to Him for help, He spoke to the storm, and said, "Quiet down!" The winds and waves subsided and all was calm.

The biggest and most destructive storm in my life was an unhappy marriage. Divorce came like thunder and a bolt of lightning which were frightening for a while, but at the same time the storm broke and cleared the air. When it happened, every area of my life was changed; no stone was left unturned.

I, too, had run frightened to Jesus. He didn't instantly calm my storm. Better yet, He calmed me. And He directed me through each individual bolt of lightning, each time teaching me more about Himself and increasing my faith.

When I was still living in an unhappy marital situation, I used to read verses in the Bible which talked about trials and difficulties. Sometimes I would get very discouraged. It sounded so easy to be strong and patient, but it wasn't all that easy for me.

In James 1: 2, 3 (TLB), for example, I'd read, "Dear brothers, is your life full of difficulties and temptations? Then be happy, for when the way is rough, your patience has a chance to grow." "Be happy?" I'd think, and wonder, "Can anyone really be happy when life is so difficult?"

That was about fifteen years ago. I began to seriously pray for patience and long-suffering. I knew I could lose my temper easily, and I was anxious to become a more patient person. But for weeks I prayed and prayed for patience, yet I saw no great changes.

Shortly thereafter, I became an enthusiastic reader of Catherine Marshall's books. I was delighted at the opportunity to hear her speak at Wheaton College, and I read all of her books. The one which was most encouraging to me was *Beyond Ourselves*.

After reading her chapter on "Ego Slaying," I thought about it for a long time. In that chapter, Catherine Marshall shares her experiences at a retreat which included a discussion of the God-centered personality versus the egocentric personality. She quotes Sheldon Turner, a lawyer who was lay leader of the retreat: "The Christ of the Cross isn't going to become real to you until you come to terms with this hard core of reality at the heart of Christianity. How could He be real to you when you — not He — are still at the center of your life?"

Turner warned the group, however, that they had better not tell God that they desired ego-slaying unless they meant it. "For no one can predict what painful experiences God will allow in order to make the experience real."

After giving it a lot of thought, I had a strong desire to ask God to take me this next step in my Christian experience. But I was afraid. What if God wanted more of me than I was willing to give?

I reminded myself that God is a loving Father and knows better than I what would make my life more meaningful. I also worried that God would require me to become a puppet or a carbon copy of every other Christian. Again, when I thought about what God is really like, I quickly realized that His plans for us are far more fulfilling and creative than any we could plan for ourselves.

Egocentricity in our personalities causes our lives to center around our own desires and self-ambitions. It drives us to want to accumulate possessions and to want others to admire and praise us. The Bible reminds us that those things do not result in either our own happiness or the accomplishment of God's purposes. And the more egocentric we are, the less able we are to bear our difficulties. We feel sorry for ourselves, become critical of others whose lives seem to run smoother, and have easily hurt feelings.

I decided that I wanted Jesus to be the focal point in my life! I wanted to do His will, not mine. So I decided to take the risk and ask God to slay my natural self.

According to Catherine Marshall, the next step was to accept by faith the fact that God heard the prayer. I accepted it all right, but many times I wondered whether I really did want to get rid of my selfish desires. They were so much a part of me! I actually enjoyed them.

In Catherine Marshall's words, "There will be a crisis or series of crises. We live through them step by step."

Divorce initiated my series of crises. And the Lord did lead me, step by step. Often I had no idea how He would help me solve a dilemma, but each time, in His own time, He directed my steps.

Looking back now through the years, I can say, "How like God to replace some of my selfish desires for happiness and material possessions with a desire for His love." And how like Him to fill me with joy till "my cup runneth over." But everything wasn't all that clear when I was living through it. At the time, so many things that happened seemed to be so endless and so exhausting. But God was working in spite of me.

In skimming through my prayer notebook for the past five years, I can go from one crisis situation to another.

Shortly after returning from camp and getting my new job, I found out we would have to move. Our landlord was putting the house we were renting up for sale. I prayed and fasted but couldn't seem to locate the right place. Actually, we wanted to stay in the same area in order not to have to transfer schools, but there were no rentals available. At the time, we were discouraged; but looking back now, from this vantage point, I realize God was leading us in a particular direction.

The time came for Pam and me to leave for Texas to attend a youth convention at the Astrodome. I had so hoped that we'd be moved and settled before the trip, but the timing wasn't right yet.

The day we returned, I read an ad in the newspaper about a house for rent in a nearby town. It sounded good, so I called and we went to look at it. We knew immediately that we wanted it. Eventually we discovered that we enjoyed this new community even more than the last; the neighbors were great and the teachers were outstanding.

Again, in retrospect, it was easier to understand why God delayed our finding a place to move. The house we rented was owned by a young couple who had just moved into it early that spring. Then, without notice, his company had transferred him to New Jersey. So their home wasn't even available for rent when we began our search.

"Now, at least we are settled," I thought. I had a job I enjoyed and we were renting a house we loved. Things were looking up.

Then, like a top, our life started spinning again. With a paper shortage and energy crisis putting many small companies out of business, I learned that the magazine I edited was one of the casualties.

The notations in my prayer notebook the following morning indicated my shock. I just couldn't believe it! Not two times in two years! But I finally realized that if God had pulled us through this kind of situation once, He could and would do it again. So I continued to pray and fast.

It was harder this time, though, to be out of work.

It was winter, close to Christmas, and the economic situation of the country was making jobs scarce. Many of the publishers I called to inquire about jobs indicated that they were laying off employees instead of hiring.

I began to panic again! As I've mentioned, I have a rather short memory when it comes to remembering the situations in which the Lord has rescued and guided me. But then I got down to brass tacks, committed the situation to the Lord, fasted and started answering want ads. I phoned friends in the business and numerous publishing houses, but nothing turned up.

Looking back, it seems unbelievable to me how blind I was to God's direct leading. Just two days after learning that my magazine was being discontinued, I received a phone call from Ferdi Pauls, a good friend. (We had worked together at the publishing house where I first started out.) He wanted to tell me about an opening for an editor at the religious publishing house where his wife, Florence, was employed as an editor. He was very enthusiastic about this opportunity. I thanked him for thinking of me, but mentioned that since this company was located 26 miles from our home, I'd have to give it some serious thought.

He encouraged me to at least go out for an interview. After our conversation ended, my first reaction was, "Now I'll have to drive all the way out there for an interview or I will really hurt his feelings." So I did phone for an interview and drove out a few days later.

Because I didn't recognize this as the opportunity God was providing, I was very casual during the interview, giving the impression, I'm sure, that I really couldn't care less if the position were offered to me or not. This was, of course, before I began my campaign to phone every publishing house in the phone book.

Many calls and interviews later, I fully realized what a good opportunity this company was offering. I decided I'd better call back and explain to the editorial director that I was really much more interested in the position than I had conveyed. Perhaps it was an urgency in my voice or anger at myself for not being more aware of the potential of the position. At any rate, my call didn't make a very good impression on the editorial director. In fact, I evidently did a pretty good job of convincing him that I'd be about the last person he'd want to hire for this job. By the time our conversation was concluded, I was discouraged. His "Well, we'll let you know our decision" sounded very ominous.

My whole world was looking very gray about then. During this period of time, prior to Christmas, while I was unemployed, I was financially wiped out. But deep within I had held onto my belief that God would provide for my family in this need as He had in the past. He must have put reassurance in my heart, because up until then I did have a sense of confidence that was unusual in such a circumstance.

However, the day when my rent became due, I followed my old pattern and began to panic. My children's father had not been able to pay me any child support for weeks since he, too, was out of work. And since we had only begun renting this house a few months earlier, I had not established a credit rating where I might have felt free to request additional time.

The rent was due on Monday morning. That weekend I was so ill with swollen glands that I stayed in bed. I didn't want to spend money for a doctor and medicine; and besides, since we were new in the area, we didn't even have a family physician. In my weak and discouraged state, after phoning a few doctors who informed me that no new patients were being taken, I gave up. But I prayed like mad while I lay suffering under the covers. I was desperate.

Then the phone started ringing. First it was Judy Cline, a good friend whom I had met when Danny attended The Ark, a church-sponsored nursery school of which Judy was director. She was wondering how I was. When I told her about my swollen glands, she exclaimed, "Darlene, I have some medication that was prescribed for me which I didn't use. I'll bring it over." She kept her word and in addition brought over a homemade cake and jar of instant orange drink. The kids were delighted, and I, per her instructions, drank cups and cups of tea and instant orange drink mixture. (Later, when I did talk with a physician, he stated that the medication I took was exactly what he would have prescribed.)

So, physically I felt somewhat better, though I was still down emotionally. Then the telephone rang again. This time it was Florence Pauls. I was in such a state of confusion that when she simply asked if I had heard anything about the job opening, I broke down into tears. She asked what was the matter and I sure gave her the whole list. I felt worn out physically, I did not have money for rent, the cupboards were pretty bare and my car wouldn't start!

Her reaction was amazing. "Hold on a minute," she said, "I want to talk with my husband." In five minutes she returned to the phone and said simply, "Would you mind if we came over for a while?"

"Mind? We'd be delighted. My kids would love some company," I replied. I assumed they wanted to help me get out of my depressed mood, and I needed all the help I could get. At this time, I knew Ferdi quite well, but had only met Florence on a few occasions.

I got out of bed, straightened the house just a bit and then heard their car pull up. They each walked in the door carrying a bag of groceries. After the excited "ohs" and "ahs" from my children, they said, "Now, let's sit down and talk a bit."

They had discussed my situation between themselves and had planned just what they were going to say. First of all, they announced, "We'd like to adopt you as part of our family. Would that be okay?"

Would it? We'd be thrilled!

Next, they brought up the subject of employment. "We don't think that you can honestly create a favorable impression on job interviews if you are so panic-stricken," they announced. "Therefore, we want you to relax and take your time. Find a job you will do well at and enjoy. In the meantime, when you run out of this food, we'll provide more. In addition,

152

we want to help you with your rent payment." And before I could object, they plopped a check (already written out) on my table. For once in my life I was speechless. I then told them I couldn't possibly accept it.

But they were prepared for my objections. Quietly and very sincerely they said, "It isn't from us, Darlene. It is from the Lord. Just this weekend we prayed that He would show us someone whom we could share our bonus with. And He led us to you. You can't turn down the Lord."

Well, the next morning's entry in my prayer notebook was joyful. Yes, of course, without any doubt God can and does answer our needs. He does care about our problems, no matter how large or small.

Interestingly, just about this time, I had been delving in my mind for a family devotional project that would distract my kids from our problems. After seeing a vivid film about the famines in Ethiopia, we decided to prepare a birthday present for Jesus. We wrapped up a small box with Christmas wrapping paper and put a slot in it for money. Every visitor to our home was encouraged to put in a few pennies; we also used some other methods to raise money. By the time Christmas came that year, we had raised a nice amount for the famine fund. God had not only provided us with our needs, but allowed us, in turn, to give to others much worse off than ourselves.

My job crisis was about to come to an end. Another friend came to the rescue. Jim Johnson, an author and also an instructor at Wheaton College

Graduate School in Wheaton, Illinois, had realized the predicament I was in. He felt I would be right for the job which Ferdi had suggested. So he took the time to call and put in a few hearty words of recommendation for me. Evidently he reassured the editorial director that I really wasn't an emotionally disturbed woman and actually was responsible and capable of acceptable work.

The day I finally received a call from the company, I was at the bowling alley watching my son bowl in the junior league. When my daughter took the message she didn't get it straight — whether I should come in because I was being offered the position or because I was being let down gently.

The news was good! When I arrived for the interview, I was offered the position. Needless to say, I accepted it gratefully and have felt certain ever since that it was all according to God's leading. This time He evidently had to make me wait it out since I was too stubborn to believe Him the first time. Working at this company has been more meaningful than I could have anticipated. I enjoy my co-workers and my job.

With a job, I felt that our lives were intact again, for a while. But that top hadn't stopped spinning. Things weren't going to become settled down just yet.

About two months after a joyful entry was put into my prayer notebook about my job, I made another entry. Again I was about to panic.

I received a phone call at work from my kids. "Mom," they cried, "we're going to be thrown out of this house! A man came from the real estate office and said we have to get out." I tried to calm my children down as I felt myself becoming increasingly angry.

"What is going on?" I wondered. "We have a lease and our rent is paid. Nothing has been damaged." When I contacted the realtor, my heart sank. The young couple who owned the house had been transferred back to the area. Because of the economy and other situations, his new position had been discontinued. I could understand their situation but we just weren't ready for another move. It had only been five months since we moved in, and I was still recuperating from that physical exertion. Besides, we loved the house and the neighbors and the school. It was a disappointing blow.

I asserted my right to stay the year until the lease was up. They were disappointed because that meant they'd have to rent an apartment for the remaining seven months. In addition, the wife was expecting her first baby and wanted to be in their home before the baby came. However, I knew I couldn't switch my children's school again so soon. So after a quick check with the neighborhood papers and realtors, I told them we'd have to stay until school was out.

"But why?" I wondered. "Why would God lead us to this town and this house and then allow us to be forced to move again?" Although we had signed only a one-year lease, we were under the impression that it would be renewed.

I put off serious house-hunting until the school year was over. Again I prayed very specifically that God would close the door of every house we looked at which would not be His will for us. Florence (a good friend by now) and I prayed together about my housing needs during our lunch hour.

My children's teachers reported a definite decrease in their enthusiasm at school, and we all realized that they were suffering from all the insecurities in their lives. So I felt it important that our summer be not spent entirely devoted to house-hunting, as the previous summer had been.

One evening, as we were praying, Danny said, "Mom, let's pray and ask God to help us buy a camper-trailer."

I felt immediately that I should go along with this request made by a trusting child. Besides, it sounded like a great idea to me! We entered the prayer in my notebook and prayed regularly about it.

In moments of lack of trust, I'd ask myself, "Where in the world will I ever get money for a camper-trailer?" But we continued to pray, and pretty soon we all had a confident feeling that God would answer this prayer request.

It was late winter when we first started praying for the camper-trailer. I realized that if we would get one, it would be best to have it by Memorial Day. So we added the request, "Could we have it by Memorial Day?" to our prayers.

Well, maybe we needed a sign of encouragement for the days of waiting that were to come, because God worked this request out so smoothly we all were delighted.

On my way home from work one day, I happened to make a wrong turn. I changed my route and was driving along when I noticed a tent-trailer opened up in front of a home. A private "For Sale" sign was on it. I was able to switch lanes and turn into their driveway. I looked at the trailer from my car and took down the phone number from the sign. But I didn't even bother to get out and look inside it, assuming it would be too expensive for us to seriously consider.

When I arrived at home, I put away the number. But later that evening I remembered it and decided to phone. The man asked if I had looked inside. He had added benches, etc., which didn't ordinarily come with this size trailer. I was amazed when I asked the price. It wasn't bad at all.

Well, it just so happens that I had just signed a contract to do a special project for my company. They would be giving me a retainer which was about the same amount as the price for the camper.

When I phoned the owner he said that there also were other parties interested, and the first person to bring over the money would make the deal. I went over with my check, and he had just accepted it when a man came to the door. He, too, was prepared to buy it that day.

Since I didn't have a hitch on my car yet, I couldn't take it with me. The owners volunteered to deliver it the next day, after signing the title. When I realized what day the next day was, I was overwhelmed.

The camper was delivered to our house and the title changed on a very special date: Dan's birthday. It will help us remember for a long time this answer to prayer.

That camper was a real encouragement to us. We believe it was another reassurance from God that we could trust Him with all our needs and even those special things we don't really need. We also believed that God intended us to use it that summer and not spend every moment looking for a house. So, many weekends, after first checking with our realtor and reading the newspaper want ads, we would head for our favorite camping site at our Bible camp.

We felt sure that God would find us a place to live when the time was ready. Occasionally the thought occurred to me that maybe He would let us wait to the last moment, the end of August, before giving us His direction. I didn't like that idea very much, and once or twice I prayed and pleaded with Him not to make us wait that long.

But I knew that when the time was right, He'd direct us. The only other concern I sometimes had was that I might not recognize His guidance and direction. After all, I had not recognized Ferdi's phone call as being the contact for my new job.

I continued to check out houses and apartments on my lunch hour, and Florence continued to pray with me about the situation. We were seeking God's guidance as to whether to remain in our new town or move closer to where I now worked. Pam loved her new high school, and since she was only a sophomore and already had attended two high schools, she was desperate to stay in the same area. I also realized that she had an exceptionally concerned guidance counselor who had shown special interest in her situation and would be guiding her through graduation.

She also was involved with the Young Life Club and had an equally dedicated and concerned director in this group. She was fortunate in having two mature men available for advice and encouragement. In addition, my sons loved their school and especially their teachers and principal. Tim was looking forward to PeeWee League and was active in a bowling league.

It seemed to me that I was more able to cope with the distance than they would be able to cope with another complete change of neighborhoods. But I tried very hard to be open to God's direction in the event He was leading us to move close to my work.

For days on end, friends from work would bring the daily newspaper and circle possibilities. Many lunch hours were spent with a co-worker, checking out a house. I'm sure I bored my friends to death that summer, but they were very patient and helpful.

Yet, whenever any good-sounding possibilities would arise, I felt that the Lord was slamming the door in my face. The same thing was happening weekends and evenings.

One of our biggest disappointments came as a result of an ad I placed in our neighborhood paper. I received just one response, and the woman calling was very enthusiastic. In fact, Pam knew her son as he was in one of her classes. We looked at the house and fell in love with it. It seemed perfect, on a quiet, dead-end street by a park and just the right size. Although the owners were somewhat hesitant about my being divorced, they did call a second time and asked me to come back to talk about it more. At that time, they both more or less agreed that we could rent it but wanted to think about it over the weekend. The woman asked me to call Tuesday morning.

When I called, her daughter answered. With no explanation, she stated, "My mother said to tell you we rented the house to a young couple."

We were all disappointed, especially Pam. But I tried to explain that evidently God had something else in mind for us and we shouldn't blame these owners. I knew that was hard to accept because, to be honest, I was having a rough time myself not becoming angry with the landlords.

This was a big problem. Most landlords did not want to rent to anyone with three children — especially a single mother. They'd always ask the same question, "What if you got sick? How would you pay the rent?" I felt it unfair that I would always get this question, while a man with the same number of children usually wouldn't be looked upon as being unreliable. At any rate, time was passing. Yet, God was giving me such complete confidence that He was in control of the situation that I did not panic nearly as much as before.

At one point a realtor friend, Dan, suggested we think in terms of trying to rent with an option to buy or even try to buy something on contract. Mortgage money being especially tight, he felt that possibly some sellers would agree to this arrangement. However, even with using this procedure, one thing after another kept falling through. Even on our own block.

Everyone in the neighborhood had been keeping an eye open for a house for us. Yet, right on our street was a house owned by a minister and his wife who now live in New York. They, of course, didn't know our needs. Overnight, their tenants moved out and the owners, through friends, rented it to a new family. We didn't hear about it till the morning after they rented it. We just couldn't understand why these doors kept closing in our faces.

At work, some friends were getting concerned for us. "Are you sure the Lord isn't expecting you to use your brain more?" they'd kindly ask. And my answer was definite because I felt definite: "The Lord will provide us with a house, and I must wait until He leads me to it."

No one actually said it to me, but I secretly suspected some co-workers of wondering about my mental health. Meantime the summer was almost over and we had to move by September 1. Yet the doors still kept slamming in our faces.

We decided we'd better start packing. My associate editor and her husband and other friends from work had volunteered to help us move. Ray, the Young Life director, had volunteered his help and his truck. Even my former husband was planning to help. Everything was all worked out now — except where we would move.

I still had a peaceful, confident feeling that had to have come from the Lord. There was no way that I could have handled this situation without His confidence.

About a week before we had to be moved out, I had to make a decision as to whether Pam should register at the same high school. To further complicate things, Pam had been offered the job as head waitress at a restaurant and the decision of whether she should accept it also had to be made immediately. Florence and I prayed, and we both felt the Lord was saying, "Go ahead, register her where she is." So I did, although we had no new address.

A few weeks earlier, a friend had been concerned about our situation and had used his business contacts to try to find any unlisted homes available. He ran into a situation where two boys, ages 18 and 21, owned a home. Both their parents had died, and they knew they really had to sell the house. But they had lived there all their lives and the house was full of memories. They spent the summer painting the outside yellow and had shag carpeting installed in the front room. But, for sentimental reasons, they had put off listing the house.

Our friend talked to them about our situation. They were interested but said we'd have to contact their lawyer, since the house was in estate. Their lawyer was on vacation! Our friend was leaving on his vacation the day their lawyer returned, but he found time to talk a few minutes with him. Their lawyer was not too enthused about the idea of a woman with three kids buying the house on contract. But he said the decision was really up to the boys who owned the house. That's when Pete, one of the young owners, whose signature naturally would be needed, left to go fishing in Canada. There was no way to contact him.

Time was running out. We had only one week left, and I wasn't certain whether Pete would be willing to sign for us to obtain the house, even if he did return in time. We found two possibilities in the town where I worked, vacant houses for sale on contract, but I still felt we should wait a few more days.

Pete returned the Tuesday before we had to move. The next evening, the boys and their lawyer and I met together. Finally about 11:30 we agreed on terms and things were looking better. But the boys had no place to move and felt they needed more time. *I didn't have time!* However, I still believed that if this was God's will, He could and would work out all the details in two days.

By now, I was getting very attached to these two boys. My daughter had established a friendly, brother-sister kind of relationship, and I really felt concerned about them and their future. I knew they needed some direction and encouraged them to register at the community college, since it was too late for any other type of college.

We made arrangements to help them move their furniture into some of the rooms and we, with the help of our friends, moved our big items into their house that following night. I realized what an emotional experience this was in their lives, since they had never lived anywhere else. Yet, I knew that as God was working out my situation, He also was working out theirs. Their friends had been using the house as a meeting place, and the situation was about to get out of hand. Many neighbors also were worried about the boys and their house.

After work that Friday we moved things into their basement, garage and porch. We still had loads of books, office items, toys and clothing at our old house. Pam worked at her waitress job Saturday while I cleaned the house we were leaving. Then, at 6 p.m. we began making trips with the remaining items. It was the middle of the night before we finished and then we had to drive, with our trailer-camper, up to our church camp to spend the Labor Day weekend. The boys had till Wednesday to find a new place to live and remove all their things.

The holiday weekend was rainy and not as restful as we had hoped. We were worried about Pete and John, and hoping they were able to get moved out without too much trouble. When we arrived Wednesday, however, we discovered that they still had not been able to locate an apartment. Although they had financial security, their ages discouraged landlords from renting to them.

Amazingly enough, the Lord also provided for this emergency. Florence and Ferdi were away on vacation. However, before leaving they had said, "Oh, by the way, if you run into a problem getting into your new home, we've left the key to our house for you just in case." I had replied, "Well, thanks, but I'm sure we'll be able to get in the house okay." I hadn't really realized we'd need a place to sleep; not one night, but as it turned out, three nights.

So, that Tuesday night at 11 o'clock we drove up, camper in tow, to their home. The first thing we discovered, after getting our tired selves into the house, was a note welcoming us. What a relief! Evidently they had really meant it when they had offered us their home to use.

Then, for the first few days of school we packed up the car each morning, drove back to our town and eventually returned each evening. Each day we thought, "Today we'll get into our house." But each day seemed to bring new complications.

Eventually, however, the boys found an apartment; interestingly enough, through my daughter's friends' mother. Then we had another delay until they were able to get into the apartment.

But we all survived the ordeal and are still on good terms. Pete and John stop over frequently, and I believe that knowing they could come in and talk to us and still visit their childhood home helped them adjust to their new apartment.

We just love our house. Only God could have found us a situation that meets our needs so perfectly. For one thing, we are still living on the same street, just a few blocks down. We have bedrooms upstairs and pine trees in our backyard. Our block is loaded with kids about the ages of mine. Finally, we really believe we have a secure home, and we are anxious to decorate it as time and money allow.

Again, looking back, we can see how everything was working out according to God's perfect timing. Not only did we all learn a lesson in patience and confidence; but during the summer months while we were waiting and praying, Pete and John were painting and carpeting our future home. Not only would this have been financially impossible for us at that time, but it also gave the boys time to prepare emotionally for a move.

These experiences and many more are included in

my prayer notebook as a constant witness to me that God hears our prayers and still works miracles in the lives of those who build their house on Christ, the Rock.

# 11

# Dating and Remarriage

DATING IS A WHOLE NEW BALL GAME. When I first became divorced, the very idea of dating was distasteful to me. That was the last thing I wanted to do; I preferred to spend every possible free moment with my children. In fact, in the first months I didn't even attend showers or go out for supper with the women I worked with.

Besides, the very word "dating" sounded highschoolish and somehow even bad to me.

Months went by and I was kept extremely busy working and caring for my children. Saturday nights were always spent giving baths and shampoos; Sunday afternoons (when we weren't invited to a friend's house) were taken up with washing, ironing and playing with my kids. After a while, I realized I was getting in a rut, but at that time I had no choice but to continue doing what I felt was necessary: devoting all my free time to my kids.

I had mixed emotions the first time a single male adult asked me out to dinner. I hardly knew how to act. I was very ill at ease and not much fun, I'm sure. Actually, I was worried. Would I have a problem at the end of the evening with this man? Would he assume he'd be invited in for coffee and to stay late?

After a while, I became less tense about dating and could relax and enjoy myself a bit. However, there was always that nagging fear about how my date expected the evening to end. My conservative viewpoints didn't always go over too well with men who had more liberal ideas. Sometimes, in fact, a fellow would reassure me on the first few dates that his viewpoint on sex, morality, etc., was the same as mine. Then, on about the third or fourth date I would suddenly realize he hadn't meant what he said.

In the transition back to dating it is very important that a divorced person put enough value on himself. It is very easy to fall into a situation where things can quickly get out of hand both emotionally and physically. Often a divorced person's deep needs for approval and reassurance color his objectivity.

It is so important to maintain a long-range view of one's future. I know of men and women who felt that as long as they were free again, what did it matter with whom they did what? Then, they met someone whose high morals and integrity caused them to feel guilty and ashamed of their actions. It can really cause problems to a future mate. Admitting a past track record can break up a relationship; not admitting it can cause painful guilt feelings.

Don't sell out at the first sign of loneliness. Dating

someone who has a different viewpoint than yours on sex can be an emotionally agonizing situation. In this age of sexual freedom, you may not want to be as free as the person you are dating. Yet you realize that by saying no there is a very real possibility that this person will disappear from your life.

The situation differs from that of high school and college singles in that there is the old assumption, "You've been married. You're used to sex. What have you got to lose?"

Ironically, many times a divorced woman has compromised her own standards because she cared for someone very much; then, the man turned around and decided that if she was all that available now, what had she done in the past?

Single men aren't the only ones who invite divorced women out. I discovered that when a married man is unhappy at home, the nearest divorced gal is sometimes the first one he runs to. In most cases, these are casual friendships without any real complications.

Other problems can be created when a divorced person misinterprets friendship and kindness from someone of the opposite sex as being something deeper. I remember incidents where I wasn't certain if a man was being helpful or whether he had an ulterior motive. And that ulterior motive might be something the man was not even aware of. Often it is some unconscious need which responds to the helplessness and/or freedom of a divorced woman.

I soon became very suspicious of married men who offered me help of any kind. For example, one very wet, damp morning my car just wouldn't kick over. I didn't feel free at that early hour on Saturday to ask a neighbor for help. But my seven-year-old son had gotten up at 7 a.m. to be sure he'd get to his bowling league on time. Since it only lasts a little over an hour, time was of the essence.

I decided to take Tim to the bowling alley in a cab. When we arrived, a father of one of the other young bowlers offered to drive me home and take a look at my car. On the one hand, I was relieved. This might save a costly towing charge. On the other hand, I wondered, "Does he have an ulterior motive? Will I feel obligated?" I decided to take his offer and he got my car running.

After we stood in the drizzling rain, I felt it only right to invite him into my house to wash his hands (greasy from my engine) and offer him a cup of hot coffee. All the time, however, I was wondering what my neighbors as well as this man might be thinking. I was grateful for his kindness yet worried that he, like many other men, might feel divorced women are in dire need of affection.

Sometimes a married man, while helping you out, will mention a "jealous wife." Again I usually worry. I surely don't want to be the cause of a family argument because he was being helpful.

I do find it difficult to believe that a divorced person cannot be friends with married persons of both sexes without those friendships being suspect. Naturally, I realize there is always the danger of a relationship turning into more than a casual friendship. But I'm not convinced that this is any more inevitable than with two married persons of the opposite sex.

I'm not the same person I was five years ago when I separated from my husband. Now that I have had to go it alone and have found that, with God's help, I can make it, I have definite ideas about remarriage.

To me, a very important consideration would be my reason for wanting to try marriage again. It would not be as a way out of financial problems or to be able to quit work and be a homemaker all day long. Nor would it be to find an identity as a Mrs. Somebody.

I believe that if it is God's will for me to remarry, He will send someone into my life whom I can respect and trust and love. I am still a believer in God's divine order of authority in a Christian home. As Larry Christenson points out in his book, *The Christian Family,* God should be the top authority in a home, with the husband next in line. I don't find that offensive, because I do not believe this would in any way stifle my individual personality nor limit my creativeness.

Interesting statistics indicate that among women in the same age brackets, the formerly married woman's chances of remarrying are greater than the never-married woman's chances of marrying for the first time.

Many divorced women receive help in this area of dating and remarriage from their children. Some children decide to take it upon themselves to find a new spouse for their parent, especially the one they live with. This can become pretty embarrassing if a child asks each man his mother dates, "Are you going to marry my mom?"

My daughter has pulled her own little mischievous deeds in this respect. And since she was in high school at the time, she should have known better!

Pam's biology teacher was a bachelor; he was also almost my age, and she thought he was cool. So she told him that she had this aunt who wasn't married, and she said her aunt would be coming to the school open house. Then she gave me explicit directions on why I just had to talk to her biology teacher.

I went to his classroom on the night of open house and very casually mentioned to him, "Pam really likes you. In fact, you are one of her favorite teachers." He smiled, but I also noticed he was blushing. However, I remembered she had mentioned he was kind of bashful, so I didn't think much about it.

Then he asked me, "Has she said anything else?"

I thought about it and then added, "Well, she hadn't wanted to take biology; I had talked her into it. But she says now that she's glad she's in your class."

He asked again, "Did she say anything else?"

I replied, "No!"

Then he told me about how she had told him all about her aunt, and some of her classmates had clued him into the fact that Pam was really talking about her mother and not an aunt.

Needless to say, we were both embarrassed by this time. But we decided that it really was sort of a compliment; Pam evidently thought enough of us both to try to arrange a romance.

A few months later, this biology teacher asked his class if any of the students' parents would be willing

to chaperone a field trip. He then specifically asked
Pam, "What about your aunt? Would she be willing
to go along?" Pam said she doubted it, but he suggested that she at least ask her aunt.

I wasn't sure if he really needed a chaperone or
was just teasing Pam. But when he phoned and
asked me personally, I agreed. We went on an educational hike on a wet, rainy day and walked miles
and miles along Lake Michigan. But it was lots of
fun and I enjoyed watching Pam with her classmates.

Later this teacher was kind enough to reciprocate
by taking me and my three kids to a White Sox
game. There was a fire at the game that evening, so
we had quite a bit of extra excitement. During the
confusion, some of Pam's biology classmates, who
also were attending the game, saw us and came over
to tease us all. It was an eventful evening, to say the
least.

That was the first and last time Pam ever tried to
matchmake. I think all the teasing she received might
have discouraged any future attempts.

The same child who is searching for a new spouse
for his parent might do an about-face if and when
his mom does get serious about a man. Suddenly the
child may see a prospective stepparent as a rival and
become fearful of losing his own parent. This is
especially true if the child's parents became divorced
in the first place because of the entrance of a new
person in one parent's life.

Another reason a child might react negatively
would be if the mother herself is uncertain about the
man. Her uncertainty can carry over to her child.

173

On the other hand, if she seems content and happy, eventually the child will respond to her mood and relax.

A potential stepparent must handle carefully his relationship with the child. Such a situation can be very demanding on both. It is wise to let time be a healing factor. Bringing excessive gifts and trying to buy a child's love can cause negative reactions. Instead, a future stepparent should give the child time to gain confidence in him as a person. He is still a stranger to the child and can be an overpowering force. While the child might desire a solid new family relationship, he might also fear it. This fear may become more pronounced if there are obvious signs of affection and embracing between his parent and the possible new mate. These can be very disturbing to a child.

Gestures of hostility and anger are usually pretty normal and to be expected on the part of the child. If the prospective stepparent establishes a good-natured reaction and a gentle but undemanding response, in time the child will usually come around. And while the child's outbursts may be startling, it is better that he release these emotions than keep them pent up inside.

My kids and I awoke early, in time to catch the sun coming up. What a perfect summer Sunday. We were camping at Lutherdale (our denomination's Bible camp), and ahead of us lay hours of relaxation and family fun.

Later that morning, we walked over to the chapel

174

for Sunday worship services. I caught a glimpse of a familiar face. It was Donna, a woman I had met at a retreat for single parents at the camp two years earlier. She was in the middle of a bunch of kids and laughing gaily. She caught my eye at the same time as I caught hers.

"Well, hi!" I called. "Where were you last summer? I looked for you."

"I've been busy," she laughed. "As a matter of fact, I got remarried."

The chapel bell rang and there was no time to get the details about this exciting bit of news. "I'll tell you all about it after the service," she promised.

I ushered my kids into the chapel, delighted with her obvious happiness. I could hardly wait to hear all about it.

"Those Nelsons are really quite a clan," I heard the lady sitting next to me say to her husband. Curious, I glanced to where she was nodding. There sat Donna, but she wasn't alone. A pleasant-looking man sat toward her right and an adorable tow-headed little boy sat on her lap. (I hadn't remembered her having any blond children!) To her left sat, well, sure enough, a row of nine kids of varied ages. "Each of her kids must have brought a friend," I guessed. But that didn't fit in with the comment made by the lady sitting next to me.

As soon as the worship was over, I maneuvered my way back to Donna. "I married a man I met camping two summers ago," she explained. "We live on a farm here in Wisconsin, and we are very happy." And before I could regain my composure she added, "Oh, and altogether we have ten kids."

Later, relaxing on the beach, she filled me in with the details of the whole delightful story. I was overwhelmed with the evidence of how much God loves each person and how He provides for them.

When I first met Donna a few years earlier, she was in the process of getting a divorce. Her husband had been running around with other women, and Donna was very discouraged. She had come to Bible camp with her tent-trailer to spend some time with her children. Her plans at that time were to continue with her new job at Rockford College and to begin taking courses there to earn a college degree.

Little did she realize that God had better plans for her. She met her new husband while he, too, was out camping with his six children. It was thrilling to see how God had worked out the situation.

In Wisconsin there was a divorced farmer, concerned because his six children were living with a mother who spent more time in bars with a variety of men than with her children. Yet, legally, as long as he was not remarried, he had little chance of obtaining custody of his children, even though he could provide a stable home for them. Meanwhile, in Illinois a woman with four children was struggling to provide a good home and also attend college.

During this time, Mr. Nelson had an elderly mother in Wisconsin who was diligently praying for her six grandchildren. She had been a dedicated Christian for years; in fact, she was the stalwart of the small country church to which she belonged. She worried about her grandchildren and continued to pray for them.

Her son went to his minister and asked, "Where can a Christian man go to find a wife?" His pastor didn't really know the answer. But God did and was working it all out in His own time and way.

After Donna met Bill, she soon realized she was falling in love with this man. She wondered how to tell her children. How would they react? She had barely started discussing the situation with them when her son said, "Mom, if you let him go, you'll never find another man like him."

Donna and Bill started making plans to get married. Donna put her house in Illinois up for sale, and again God worked everything out. It not only sold for the right price, but the new buyers wanted to get in just at the right time — shortly after Donna's wedding.

Dating across state lines wasn't too easy. Each Sunday they would all attend church together. Every other Sunday Donna would drive up to Wisconsin, and after church they would spend the day together — snowmobiling in the winter, picnicking in the summer. The alternate Sundays he would drive down to Illinois with his children for dinner, all worshiping at her church.

Soon after they were married and settled on the farm, they started proceedings to gain custody of his children. Since their mother didn't really want to be bothered by them anyway, everything went smoothly. She had been neglecting them and not even giving them routine care.

The grandmother lived to see her prayers answered.

All ten children visited her at a nursing home on her last birthday. She was overjoyed. Only a short time later she passed away, having lived long enough to see her son and his family happy again.

The farm was another blessing for Donna and her children. One of the first things she did when she became a farmer's wife was to plant a large garden. She agreed to do the planting and canning; the kids were responsible for tending the garden. Their father would hand one kid a hoe, tell him to "hoe a row" and then pass the hoe on the next day to the next child in line.

One day, when the kids were complaining mildly about having to "do so much work," Bill decided to show them what real work was. They spent an entire Saturday cleaning the barn and yard. The kids all fell asleep early that night, and it was the last time any complaints were heard about too much work. Bill has assumed the proper authority and discipline, combined with love and concern, and the kids all respect him for that.

Their families have blended better than even Donna and Bill expected. Living on a farm has helped tremendously. As parents, they are active in 4-H work and also teach Sunday school. Donna's oldest son will be ready for college soon and will attend Whitewater Teacher's College, a branch of the University of Wisconsin. He'll be able to live on the farm while he attends school, thus solving another problem. Donna can also resume studies at Whitewater College.

When the Nelson clan want to go someplace together, they have to take two cars. Donna laughed as she explained that, while she usually drives the youngest and smallest kids, she has the bigger car. Her husband and the big teenagers pile into a small compact car.

Donna was quick to emphasize that seeing how God worked everything out has been a really strengthening experience to her own faith as well as her husband's. Whenever a problem, be it financial or whatever, arises, she simply says, "Don't worry. God has brought us this far. I don't believe He plans to desert us now."

They both realize how wonderfully God has answered their prayers and showered His love on their family of twelve. All agree they have never been happier nor their faith stronger.

# Helpful Organizations

Check with your local phone book or neighborhood newspaper for area addresses:

Al-Anon Family Groups
P.O. Box 182
Madison Square Garden
New York, NY 10010
There are local chapters which meet regularly to help people who must deal with the effects of another's alcoholism.

Al-A-Teens
(contact through Al-Anon)
This is a support group
    for teenaged relatives
    and friends of alcoholics

Alcoholics Anonymous
Contact through local churches,
    phone books, etc.

America's Society of Divorced Men
575 Keep Avenue
Elgin, IL 60120

Catholic Charities Counseling Centers

Church Federations-Pastoral Care Institutes

Community Referral Services

Family Service Bureaus

Legal Aid Bureau

Lutheran Family Services

Mental Health Centers and Clinics (state)

National Organization for Women

Parents Without Partners

Pastoral Counseling Centers

Salvation Army Family Service Divisions

United Charities Family Service Bureau

# Helps

For lists of professional marriage counselors of varying backgrounds and religious beliefs, contact:

American Association of Marriage
   Counselors, Inc.
270 Park Avenue
New York, New York

American Association of Marriage and Family
   Counselors (AAMFC)
225 Yale Avenue
Claremont, CA 91711

Association of Christian Marriage Counselors
5051 North Central Park Avenue
Chicago, IL 60625

The Child Welfare League, Inc.
24 West 40th Street
New York, New York (child guidance agencies)

Christian Association
   for Psychological Studies
6850 Division Avenue, South
Grand Rapids, MI 49508

FAITH AT WORK
P.O. Box 1790
Waco, TX 76703 (weekend conferences,
   pamphlets, study guides)

The Family Service Association of America
192 Lexington Avenue
New York, New York (for family agencies)

MOMMA (a monthly newspaper)
P.O. Box 5759
Santa Monica, California

The National Alliance for Family Life, Inc.
  (NAFL, INC.)
10727 Paramount Boulevard
Downey, CA 90241

The National Association
  for Mental Health, Inc.
1790 Broadway
New York, New York (for psychiatric clinics
  or qualified psychiatrists)

Organization of Christian Counseling
  Centers and Counselors
342 Madison Avenue
New York, NY 10017

# Pamphlets

*Divorce Lifeline*
% Rev. Neal Kuyper
1013 Eighth Avenue
Seattle, WA 98104

*Guidelines of Discrimination Because of Sex*
Department of Labor, Equal Employment
  Opportunity Commission (EEOC)
100 Charles River Plaza
Boston, MA 02114

*Pre-school Observation Guide*
Division of Continuing Education
University of Massachusetts
Amherst, MA 01002
Single copies, 75¢; ten or more, 50¢ each.
Developed in response to a need of parents
of young children for some clear
criteria to use in deciding what preschool
is best for their children.

*Professional Women and Academic Women's
  Organization*
For the list of an up-to-date roster, write to:
Bernice Sandler,
Association of American Colleges
Project on the Status and Education of Women
1818 R. Street N.W.
Washington, DC 10009

*Sex Discrimination in Employment, What to Know
About It, What to Do About It*
$1.50
National Organization for Women
45 Newbury Street
Boston, Massachusetts

# Recommended Reading List

Bach, George R. and Wyden, Peter. *The Intimate Enemy*. New York: William Morrow, 1969.

Crook, Roger H. *An Open Book to the Christian Divorcee*. Nashville: Broadman Press, 1974.

Despert, Juliette Louise. *Children of Divorce*. Garden City: Doubleday, Dolphin Books, 1962.

Dodson, Fitzhugh. *How to Parent*. Los Angeles: Nash, 1970.

Dodson, Fitzhugh. *How to Father*. Los Angeles: Nash, 1973.

Hollett, Kathryn. *A Guide for Single Parents*. Transactional Analysis for People in Crisis. Milbrae, Calif.: Celestial Arts, 1974.

Howe, Louise Kapp. *The Future of the Family*. New York: Simon and Schuster, 1972.

Hudson, Lofton R. *'Til Divorce Do Us Part*. Nashville: Thomas Nelson, 1973.

Hunt, Morton M. *The World of the Formerly Married*. New York: McGraw-Hill, 1966.

Krantzler, Mel. *Creative Divorce*. New York: Signet, New American Library, 1975.

Maltz, Maxwell. *Psycho-Cybernetics*. New York: Pocket Books, 1960.

McFadden, Michael. *Bachelor Fatherhood*. New York: Walker, 1974.

O'Brien, Patricia. *The Woman Alone*. New York: Quadrangle, 1973.

O'Neill, Nena and O'Neill, George. *Shifting Gears*. New York: Evans, 1974.

Parker, Rolland S. *Emotional Common Sense*. New York: Harper & Row, 1973.

Steinzor, Bernard. *When Parents Divorce*. New York: Pantheon, 1969.

Stewart, Suzanne. *Divorced*. Grand Rapids: Zondervan, 1974.

Vayhinger, John. *Before Divorce*. Philadelphia: Fortress. 1972.

*If you've just finished this book, we think
you'll agree . . .*

## A COOK PAPERBACK IS

# REWARDING READING
### Try some more!

## (Cont.)

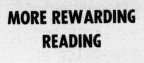

**WHAT ABOUT HOROSCOPES?** by Joseph Bayly. A topic on everyone's mind! As the author answers the question posed by the title, he also discusses witches, other occult subjects.
51490—95¢

**IS THERE HEALING POWER?** by Karl Roebling. A keen interest in healing led the author to a quest of facts. A searching look at faith healers: Kathryn Kuhlman, Oral Roberts, others.
68460—95¢

**SEX SENSE AND NONSENSE** by James Hefley. Just what does the Bible say, and NOT say, about sex? A re-examination of common views—in the light of the Scriptures.
56135—95¢

**THE KENNEDY EXPLOSION** by E. Russell Chandler. An exciting new method of lay evangelism boosts a tiny Florida church from 17 to 2,450 members. Over 50,000 copies sold.
63610—95¢

**STRANGE THINGS ARE HAPPENING** by Roger Ellwood. Takes you for a close look at what's happening in the world of Satanism and the occult today . . . and tells what it means.
68478—95¢

———————

You can order these books from your local bookstore, or from the David C. Cook Publishing Co., Elgin, IL 60120 (in Canada: Weston, Ont. M9L 1T4).

-------------**Use This Coupon**-------------

Name _____

Address _____

City _____ State _____ ZIP Code _____

| TITLE | STOCK NO. | PRICE | QTY. | ITEM TOTAL |
|-------|-----------|-------|------|------------|
|       |           | $     |      | $          |
|       |           |       |      |            |
|       |           |       |      |            |
|       |           |       |      |            |
|       |           |       | Sub-total | $     |

**NOTE:** On orders placed with David C. Cook Publishing Co., add handling charge of 25¢ for first dollar, plus 5¢ for each additional dollar.

. . . . . . . . . . . . Handling

TOTAL $ _____